University of London
Institute of Commonwealth Studies

COMMONWEALTH PAPERS

General Editor
Professor W. H. Morris-Jones

15
Whitehall and the Colonial Service:
An Administrative Memoir, 1939–1956

COMMONWEALTH PAPERS

Whitehall and the Colonial Service: An Administrative Memoir, 1939-1956

by

CHARLES JEFFRIES

*formerly Joint Deputy Under-Secretary
of State, Colonial Office*

UNIVERSITY OF LONDON
Published for the
Institute of Commonwealth Studies
THE ATHLONE PRESS
1972

Published by
THE ATHLONE PRESS
UNIVERSITY OF LONDON
at 4 Gower Street, London WC1

Distributed by Tiptree Book Services Ltd
Tiptree, Essex

U.S.A. and Canada
Humanities Press Inc
New York

© *University of London* 1972

ISBN 0 485 17615 7

C

Printed in Great Britain by
WESTERN PRINTING SERVICES LTD
BRISTOL

FOREWORD

This book is the first of its kind in the *Commonwealth Papers* series. Its inclusion is an indication of the Institute's interest not only in the period of decolonization and transfer of power but also in encouraging the writing of memoirs by men with special administrative experience of these processes. By any standard British decolonization represents a phase of exceptional change, important to an understanding of the recent history of this country and of the new states alike. The documents of the time will, as they become available, permit historians to unravel the elements and reconstruct the processes but there are contributions of special value which are available only from those who were directly involved. Such men may have assisted in steering Whitehall through its readjustments or they may have worked in the adaptations called for in the administrations of new states. In either case they have precious stories to tell.

The Institute wishes to thank The Nuffield Foundation for their interest in work of this kind and for the grant which they made to facilitate this particular publication.

W.H.M-J.

AUTHOR'S PREFACE

In *The Colonial Empire and its Civil Service*, published by Cambridge University Press in 1938, I recorded the history of the British Colonial Service up to that date and described the contemporary state and organization of the Service. In *Partners for Progress* (Harrap, 1949) I tried to give a picture of the Service as it stood in the years immediately following the second world war, and in *The Colonial Police* (Parrish, 1952) I dealt in some detail with the work of that particular branch of the Service.

Many members of the Colonial Service have recorded their first-hand experiences, and distinguished authorities have written about the methods by which the Service was recruited, the kinds of people who made up the Service, and the constitutional position of civil servants in the colonial governments. So far, however, no account has been given of the problems of organization and management which arose in connection with the Colonial Service in the period of 'decolonization'. The official files will in due course be available to the student but files cannot tell the whole story and, having been intimately concerned with the administration of the Colonial Service from 1930 to 1956, I can write of these matters from personal recollection.

I could not have accomplished this task without much encouragement and help from others. I should like especially to thank Viscount Boyd of Merton, Professor W. H. Morris-Jones, Mr J. M. Lee, Mr B. Cheeseman, Mr C. de Castro and other members of the Library and Records Department of the Foreign and Commonwealth Office, Mr A. R. Thomas, Mr A. E. Drake, Mr J. R. Symonds, Sir Bernard Braine, MP, Sir Christopher Cox, and Mr T. E. Smith.

CONTENTS

PROLOGUE

In the nineteen-twenties the British Colonial Empire—leaving aside the self-governing Dominions, India, and Burma—was, in terms of size and extension throughout the world, at its highest peak. The historian of the future will probably see the British colonial adventure as an important but brief and uncharacteristic episode in the epic of the nation. The British have always been interested in trade, and from the sixteenth to the twentieth centuries they were interested in breaking out of their small islands to found settlements in the more or less unpeopled regions of the temperate zones. They have not been imperialists in the sense of seeking to impose their rule upon subject populations. When they have imposed their rule it has not generally been for the sake of glory or domination but because the furtherance of their main interests appeared to make such action necessary.

At the end of the first world war, mandates from the League of Nations added responsibility for the administration of Iraq, Palestine, Tanganyika, and other smaller ex-German territories to the existing parish of the Secretary of State for the Colonies, which already included huge areas of East, West, and Central Africa, the Malay Peninsula, Ceylon, the West Indies, and innumerable islands, large and small, distributed about the Atlantic, Pacific, and Indian Oceans and the Mediterranean Sea. Under a variety of constitutional forms fifty or so* separate administrative units, covering a land area of two million square miles, with a population of fifty million, were subject to the sovereignty or authority of the British Crown, and the Secretary of State was the Minister responsible for advising the Crown and for conveying the directions of the Crown to the local administrations. The Colonial Office was the secretariat provided to assist the Secretary of State in carrying out his duties: to furnish him with the necessary information on matters requiring decision and to translate his decisions into appropriate action.

To state these facts, however, cannot go far to satisfy anyone who is concerned to discover not only what happened but why things happened as they did and not otherwise. The student of colonial (or any other) administration wishes to know where the real seat of power

* To state an exact figure would involve discussion of the definition of a 'unit'.

was to be found; where and by whom decisions were actually taken; on what grounds they were based; by what pressures they were influenced; what alternative options were in fact open to the decision-maker. It is obvious that an individual Minister, holding office for at best a few years and without necessarily any previous knowledge of the work of his Department, could not possibly, however able and industrious he might be, deal directly and personally with the vast number of questions involved in the government of the territories under his charge. There had to be much delegation of authority, both to the Governors and legislative bodies in the territories and to the experienced civil servants in the Colonial Office itself. Where did such delegation begin and end? Where was the line drawn between policy and executive action? How far were events the automatic outcome of the working of 'the system' or determined by the activity or in-activity of individual Ministers or officials? Was there indeed a 'system', or were the Secretary of State and his officials unable to do much more in practice than react as best they could to a series of crises?

Such questions as these are essential to the understanding of history, but they cannot be answered in the abstract. They can be usefully considered only in relation to some specific sphere of action; it may be that, even if the enquiry were limited to the work of the Colonial Office, different answers would result from examination of different aspects of the Office's activities. Nevertheless, the case history of one aspect, if it does not afford full illumination, can at least throw light upon the general picture.

One of the principal activities of the Colonial Office, especially from the nineteen-twenties onwards, was the management of the Colonial Service. It was a cardinal feature of British colonial administration from the early days that the Secretary of State had entire control of the appointment of persons to all but the most subordinate official posts (that is to say, junior clerks, artisans, messengers, police constables, and the like) in the territories under his jurisdiction. With one import-ant exception (the 'Eastern Cadet' Civil Services of Ceylon, Malaya, and Hong Kong, which from 1869 onwards were filled by open com-petitive examination), all appointments were under his 'patronage'. The selection of candidates from outside the territories to what became known as the Colonial Service remained the personal prerogative of the Secretary of State until 1930, but long before then it had become established practice that, when senior posts in the colonies became vacant, officials of the Colonial Office would review the records and qualifications of officers already in the Service and make recommen-dations to the Secretary of State for filling the vacancies by promotion or transfer. To some extent, therefore, there existed, from 1900 or so onwards, the rudiments of a centrally managed Service, but it is essential to the understanding of the events to be described in this book to bear in mind that at all times the public service of each administrative unit of the colonial Empire was constitutionally a separate and self-contained entity, and that every officer of the so-called Colonial Service was in fact in the employment of one or other of the territorial governments and not in any sense in the employment or pay of the United Kingdom government, the Colonial Office, or the Secretary of State. This had little practical significance so long as the United Kingdom government effectively controlled the financial and administrative operations of the colonial governments, and the officers of the higher administrative and professional grades, mostly recruited from Britain, were *de facto* the agents of the Imperial authority. The anomaly of their constitutional position became progressively a more important factor in the situation as the colonial territories moved towards a greater degree of self-government, leading to eventual independence. The question of strategy then posed was whether the idea of a managed Service should be abandoned and the public services of the territories left to develop individually along their own lines or whether the British government should itself undertake the provision of a managed Service to meet the continuing needs of the territories for skilled staffs recruited from outside.

The theme of this book is the endeavour of the Colonial Office to find an answer to this question in the continually changing circumstances of the period between 1930, when the principle of 'unification' of the Colonial Service was officially accepted, and 1960, after which date the residual functions of the Colonial Office in regard to what was by then known as Her Majesty's Overseas Civil Service were transferred to the newly created Department of Technical Co-operation.

The problem of devising a general strategy was immensely complicated by the wide variety of tactical situations in individual territories differing, as they did, so greatly in their economic, social, and geographical circumstances and their ability to be self-supporting. The conflicting forces at work can, however, be broadly stated. On the one hand, the general economic and social development of the colonial territories, deliberately accelerated by the British government through the operation of the Colonial Development and Welfare Acts from 1940 onwards, called for the employment of large and highly qualified administrative, professional, and technical staffs which could not, for the most part, be provided at that stage from the populations of the territories themselves. The recruitment, training, and deployment of these staffs was a major responsibility of the Colonial Office. On the other hand, political development in many of the territories and the increasing pressure for self-government which surged up almost every-where after the end of the war, led to growing resistance on the part of political leaders in the colonies to dictation from without as to what officers should be employed and on what terms, and to demands that expatriate staffs should be withdrawn as quickly as local candidates could be found to take their places, even though this should entail loss of efficiency.

The official statements issued by the British government from time to time show what action was taken in the attempt to reconcile these forces, but they naturally give little indication of the alternative options which were considered or of the extent to which room for manœuvre really existed. The first ten years after the unification of the Colonial Service in 1930 were spent in organizing the unified Service. The officials of the Colonial Office and the Governors of the colonies collaborated in working out the schemes, and the constitutional position in relation to most of the territories was such that once decisions had been taken there was no real difficulty in putting them into effect. It was a fairly straightforward administrative exercise.*

The outbreak of war and the passage of the first Colonial Development and Welfare Act in 1940 introduced a new phase. The prospect of intensified recruitment and expansion after the war indicated the need for much more active initiative, direction, and co-ordination on the part of the Colonial Office. At the same time, the already apparent trend towards meeting the growing desire of the peoples of the colonies to be allowed a more effective voice in the running of their affairs favoured a relaxation rather than a strengthening of central control from Whitehall. The dilemma remained unresolved until, by the early nineteen-fifties, the rapid progress of some of the more important territories towards self-government had given rise to a strong feeling of insecurity in the minds of the expatriate members of the local civil services. This not only hampered recruitment but threatened the territories with an exodus of their experienced staffs just at the time when those staffs were most needed to enable them to develop a viable government and a viable economy for their future role as independent states.

The Colonial Office was now faced with a dual problem: how to provide acceptable guarantees for expatriate officers in career posts when constitutional development towards independence had got under way; and how to re-shape the structure of the Service so as best to meet the continuing needs of the territories for skilled assistance. Both aspects of the problem involved consideration of the extent (if any) to

*A detailed account is contained in my book, *The Colonial Empire and its Civil Service* (Cambridge, 1938).

which the United Kingdom government should accept financial as well as moral responsibility for whatever solutions might be devised. This brought the Treasury and other departments into the argument, and the eventual decisions were taken not in the Colonial Office but at the highest political level.

The discussions and negotiations can be seen, in retrospect, to have fallen into three sections. The first section covers the years 1941 to 1944, during which the Colonial Office was working out plans for the post-war organization of the Service. The second round of negotiations started about 1947, when it had become clear that political changes in the territories called for a re-examination of the constitutional position of colonial civil servants. This section was marked by successive efforts to solve the problem of providing the civil servants with adequate guarantees of career and security of tenure while at the same time progressively withdrawing Whitehall's effective control over the internal affairs of the colonial governments. No satisfactory solution emerged, and by 1953 it was recognized that a new structure would have to be devised within which existing staffs would be content to remain as long as they should be needed, and new staffs could be recruited as required, in order to help the territories through and beyond the transition from colonial status to independence. This led to the constitution of Her Majesty's Overseas Civil Service in 1954 and to subsequent consideration of the role and responsibility of Her Majesty's Government in the United Kingdom for that Service. These discussions came to a head in 1956, and later developments were based on the decisions of principle taken then.

When I write the 'Colonial Office', it may fairly be asked what I really mean. Was action in any given case determined by Ministers or by the permanent officials, and, if the latter, at what stage in the hierarchy? A brief account of the procedure as I knew it may not be out of place.

All official letters from the Colonial Office were stated to have been written by direction of the Secretary of State: all communications to colonial Governors went in the first person over his name. Since the latter alone numbered many thousands in a year (87,000 in 1953, for instance), only a fraction could have received his personal authorization. The interesting question is how that fraction was selected. There were, in fact very few rules. Obviously the Secretary of State had to be involved in any matter (even if it were of itself of minor importance) which came up, or was likely to come up, in Parliament by way of question or debate or which called for a public statement. It was established custom that any petition or formal representation sent through the Governor of a colony from any individual or body should be submitted, with the appropriate briefing, by the Office staff to the

Secretary of State or Parliamentary Under-Secretary. Recommendations from Governors for disciplinary action against officers of the Colonial Service were likewise submitted to Ministers for decision. If a Secretary of State wished to deal personally with any subject he would naturally make this known to the staff. For the rest, the question whether or at what stage any issue should be submitted to Ministers was determined by the judgment and experience of the civil servants dealing with it. So far as Colonial Service matters were concerned, apart from the selection of candidates for Governorships (which required a submission from the Secretary of State to the Sovereign) and for the highest administrative and judicial appointments, the day-to-day work connected with the management of the Service was very largely carried on by the officials, who knew the technicalities and the personalities. It was up to the staff to initiate plans of action which circumstances in their judgment demanded, and to carry out the preliminary enquiries and negotiations.

In discharging these duties, the Personnel, or Colonial Service, Division of the Office worked in close touch with the geographical departments and also with the Secretary of State's Advisers. The latter were distinguished experts in their own subjects (law, medicine, agriculture, education, labour, and so forth), who were on the permanent establishment of the Office. They did not exercise executive powers or take decisions, but their views carried great weight both with officials and with Ministers. There was also a network of standing advisory councils and committees which, though they were not normally concerned with Service management, were a valuable medium for bringing outside professional and public opinion into consultation. On suitable occasions the Office staff might advise the Secretary of State to appoint a special committee to investigate and report on some particular Service problem. This was often done not so much in the hope that the committee would discover a solution that had not occurred to the Office as with the object of marshalling authoritative outside support for some line of action which the staff wanted to take. The 'Devonshire' committee on training mentioned in Chapter 2 below was an excellent example of this technique. I do not, of course, mean to suggest that these committees always rubber-stamped the Office proposals or never produced ideas of their own. Looking back I feel that the Office might have been well advised to seek more of this kind of external help in dealing with the problems of the future of the Colonial Service which arose during the fifties, but the issues were perhaps not clear-cut enough and the background was changing too rapidly to enable suitable agenda to be prepared. Moreover, it would have been difficult if not impossible to proceed without giving the colonies an opportunity of being represented, and there was no machinery providing for any kind of collective representation. This was a fatal objection to the proposals often put forward for establishing some sort of colonial Advisory Council, since no territory would have been satisfied to be represented otherwise than by its own nominee, and this would have made any advisory body impracticably unwieldy.

When the Personnel Division was formed in 1930, it was organized in two departments—an Appointments Department under Major R. D. (afterwards Sir Ralph) Furse and a Colonial Service Department under myself. The head of the Division was an Assistant Under-Secretary of State, who reported to the Permanent Under-Secretary. Sir George Tomlinson served as Assistant Under-Secretary from 1930 to 1939, when I succeeded him. On becoming Permanent Under-Secretary in 1947, Sir Thomas Lloyd decided that he was not going to be a personal bottle-neck, and delegated the responsibility for certain sections of the Office work to the two Deputy Under-Secretaries. I was appointed to one of these posts, and my share included what was by then known as the Colonial Service Division, so that I was normally responsible directly to Ministers for its work, Sir Thomas being kept generally informed of what was going on and brought into discussion when any important question of policy was being considered.

By this time the Division had grown into four departments, but, while every department and individual was assigned a particular job, the whole was very much of a team. There was no special level at which decisions were taken, and initiative might and did spring from any level. In practice this informal arrangement worked extremely well, because of the very high quality of the staffs concerned.

As a rule, therefore, in writing this book I shall make it a general practice not to identify particular individuals with particular decisions or initiatives unless there seems to be a special reason for doing so, but I shall seek to indicate, so far as may be appropriate, the respective responsibilities of civil servants and Ministers both generally and in the context of particular issues.

Perhaps I should make it clear here that the following study is limited to consideration of the general policy and particular problems connected with the structure and organization of the Colonial Service. It would be quite wrong to suppose that this work, important as it was, constituted, quantitatively, a major part of the operations of the Colonial Service Division of the Colonial Office, let alone of the Office as a whole. Most of the Division, most of the time, was fully engaged in the practical work of running the Service. This involved— amongst other things—the whole apparatus of recruitment, selection, and training of candidates from outside for all branches of the Service and the organization of in-Service training; the recording, collating, and assessment of the Governors' reports on serving officers, in order that they should be properly considered for opportunities of promotion and transfer and that the best possible selection should be made in filling each vacancy that occurred; maintenance of personal contact with officers by seeing them when on leave and by visiting the colonies; drawing up codes of regulations and pension laws; looking after the affairs of officers on leave; and dealing, from day to day, with the innumerable queries and questions demanding decisions and rulings which came up on the personal files of many thousands of officers. Most matters of mere routine were dealt with by the colonial governments or, in the United Kingdom, by the Crown Agents for the Colonies. The Colonial Office was not, for example, concerned in the local posting of officers or the assignment of their duties. Such administrative matters were the responsibility of the Governors, and were handled under their direction, by the local secretariats and departmental heads. The things that came to the Colonial Office were such as needed a decision by or in the name of the Secretary of State, including questions affecting the remuneration, promotion, transfer, and discipline of officers, and the application of general regulations to individual cases. Such questions usually involved correspondence or consultation with Governors, other departments of the Office, Advisers, or all of them before the matter was settled.

To attempt to describe this large and complex body of work, though it might have some documentary value, would take me far outside the limits of the present study. I should, however, like the reader to understand that the events which I am about to record took place against the background of the main daily tasks and preoccupations of the Office staff. Whatever view the historian may take of the policies of the Colonial Office, I believe that it can justly be claimed that its practices, in the actual administration of the Colonial Service, were as fair and humane as possible, allowing for the limitations on its powers and the liability of all men and institutions to error. I can at least testify that at all times it was the will and intention of the whole staff to do their best for the members of the great Service with the management of which they had the honour to be entrusted, and through them for the benefit of the countries and peoples whose welfare the Colonial Service existed to promote.

I

THE UNIFIED SERVICE

When the second world war broke out in September 1939, the British Colonial Service appeared to be on the verge of a new era of achievement and prosperity. Since its constitution, in 1930, as a 'unified' Service, it had become, not only in theory but to a considerable extent in practice, an organized corporate body of some seven thousand men and women, enjoying a high reputation alongside the other organized civil services of the Crown. Thanks largely to the efforts of British civil servants, the colonial territories had already made very considerable social and economic progress, especially during the preceding two decades; and now, for the first time, there was a real prospect of substantial funds being made available by the British Parliament for promoting the still more rapid development of the territories and the welfare of their peoples. The politicians and public of the mother country, traditionally content to leave the colonies to make their own way in the world as best they could, had at length awakened to a serious sense of responsibility for these overseas dependencies of the Crown, and the negotiations which were to lead to the passage of the first Colonial Development and Welfare Act in 1940 were already in hand. It was possible, and indeed natural, to look forward with confidence and hope to a future in which, for an indefinitely long time, the men and women of an expanding Colonial Service would work, in fruitful partnership with the colonial peoples, to overcome, step by step, the handicaps of poverty, ignorance, and disease, and so to enable these countries to take their places as ordered and prosperous communities in the society of nations.

There was so much to be done. In most of the territories which made up the British colonial empire the condition of the general population was comparable to that of the European peoples many centuries earlier. It was assumed that with twentieth-century knowledge and resources the process of their social evolution could be telescoped, but at best it would need much time, much patience, much labour, much money, and, above all, peace.

How far such forecasts would have been proved accurate if peace had been vouchsafed, no one will ever know. The six years of war which were to follow inevitably set back the programme in many of its practical aspects. It was perhaps less seen at the time to be inevitable that the effect of the war was so to undermine the whole concept and philosophy of 'colonialism' that the advance of the territories towards political independence would race far ahead of social and economic development. Paradoxically, therefore, the Colonial Service needed to be continually expanded to meet new and pressing demands for the skills and leadership which its members could contribute while, at the same time, as an institution, it was rapidly declining into an anachronism.

The total strength of the Colonial Service, taking the term to cover all the civil servants of all ranks in the employment of all the colonial governments, was of the order of 200,000 at the beginning of the second world war and 300,000 by the mid-fifties. The great majority of these were locally domiciled and locally recruited. The Colonial Office was concerned with them only to a limited extent. Rates of pay and other conditions of service were fixed by the colonial governments and, although the expenditure involved needed the Secretary of State's approval, the Colonial Office did not normally intervene with regard to the details. The Governors' appointments of persons from outside or inside the public service to fill posts in all but the lowest grades were also subject to the Secretary of State's approval, but this was usually a formality, disposed of through a quarterly return. All civil servants, however humble, had a right of appeal to the Secretary of State, through the Governor, if they felt aggrieved. This right was quite freely exercised and the petitions were very carefully examined in the Colonial Office. In most cases the result was that the Secretary of State saw no good reason to intervene.

The unification of the Service which had been effected in 1930 was a compromise. Until 1930 there was officially no Colonial Service as such. Each administrative unit for which the Secretary of State for the Colonies was responsible had its own public service, paid for from its revenues according to votes of its legislature, and subject to its laws and regulations. Officers were appointed to their posts by the Governor. He, however, was obliged to follow the directions of the Crown, as conveyed by the Secretary of State, in making appointments to all but purely subordinate posts. In practice, the Secretary of State not only recruited and nominated candidates from outside to fill vacancies, but could, if he thought fit, offer a post in one territory to an officer already serving in another. This 'patronage' work was traditionally dealt with in the Secretary of State's private office by his private secretaries. Their numbers had been increased to handle the spate of recruitment after the first world war, and, as it became the custom for successive Secretaries of State to reappoint the same team, they had developed into an experienced and efficient recruiting organization. In the General Department of the Colonial Office itself there was a section in which the records and confidential reports of serving officers were collated, so that, when vacancies in senior posts were notified by Governors, possible candidates from all the territories could be considered.

The decision to effect a formal unification of the Colonial Service was not due to a bureaucratic urge for tidiness or to pressure from the colonial governments or their staffs. It was due, primarily, to the fact that the growing needs of the territories for well-qualified and carefully selected candidates covering a wide range of professional and technical disciplines could not be adequately met under the existing system. Suitable candidates in sufficient numbers could not be attracted unless they could be offered the prospect of a career not necessarily limited to any one territory and could be assured that they would be serving under the general supervision and protection of the British government, represented by the Secretary of State. Nor could the needs of the territories be properly provided for unless the Secretary of State was in a position to deploy the available personnel to the best advantage. These considerations were strongly pressed upon the Colonial Office from 1920 onwards by authoritative bodies concerned with important professional branches such as medicine, education, agriculture, forestry, and veterinary science, but they applied also to the administrative and other services. The need for action was urged upon successive Secretaries of State by Major Furse, the principal Private Secretary for appointments. The Office, however, organized on a geographical basis and geared to dealing with the colonies individually, was not really equipped to initiate general action of the kind that the situation required.

In 1925 the Colonial and Dominions Offices were separated, and a colonial Governor, Brigadier-General Sir Samuel Wilson, was appointed Permanent Under-Secretary of State in the Colonial Office. He, the Secretary of State (Mr L. S. Amery), and the Parliamentary Under-Secretary (Mr W. G. A. Ormsby-Gore, afterwards Lord Harlech) were all convinced of the need both for unification of the colonial services and for closer integration of the Colonial Office itself with those services and, in spite of the conservative attitude adopted by most of the senior permanent staff, decided that reorganization was necessary. The task of advising on the form which that reorganization should take was entrusted in 1929 to an authoritative committee presided over by Sir Warren Fisher, Permanent Secretary of the Treasury and Head of the Home Civil Service. The committee's report was considered and supported by a conference of colonial Governors in the summer of 1930. The Secretary of State (then Lord Passfield) accepted the principle of unification as recommended by the committee and endorsed by the Governors, and it was put into operation on 1 October 1930.

The principle, as adopted, fell short of some hopes. The idea which Sir Samuel Wilson had cherished of integrating the Colonial Office with the Colonial Service had to be dropped, as did any idea that the Colonial Service should be directly employed and administered by the British government. Such ideas were repugnant to the Treasury. Nevertheless, official recognition was now given to the existence of a single Colonial Service which would be divided into a series of functional branches (administrative, agricultural, legal, medical, and so on). A Personnel Division was set up in the Colonial Office to deal with recruitment and the general management of the Service and to work out the practical implications of the policy of unification. The function, hitherto performed by the Private Secretaries, of recommending candidates to the Secretary of State for first appointment to the Service, was entrusted to an impartial Colonial Service Appointments Board, associated with the Civil Service Commissioners.

The Colonial Office was directly concerned only with the management of the higher administrative, professional, and technical grades of the colonial public services. Before 1930 the definition of posts within the Secretary of State's 'patronage' was fixed with reference to their salaries. After 1930 the Secretary of State's control extended both over posts carrying certain salaries and over posts, irrespective of salary, included in the schedules of the unified branches. A rough count was made from time to time of the numbers of officers covered by these definitions. In 1938 the total number of officers serving in the grades controlled by the Secretary of State was estimated at about 7,000. This figure included about 1,500 administrative officers, 600 medical, 400 police, 300 legal, and 300 agricultural.

The first need was to give some definite content to the unified Service, that is to determine to whom unification should apply and what this signified in terms of privileges and obligations. There was no question of doing away with the established system under which the actual employers of officers were the Colonial governments. Unification would never have been agreed to if that had been proposed. It was to be superimposed upon, not to replace, the existing organization. The solution to this problem worked out in the Personnel Division was to draw up, for each functional branch, a schedule of posts which would normally be filled by members of that branch of the unified Service, that is to say, posts which required certain educational or professional qualifications and for which persons would not normally be available in the population of the territory concerned.

The holders of these scheduled posts on the date on which the scheme was brought into force for any branch would automatically be listed as members of that branch. After the appointed date, membership of a branch would be conferred on an individual (with his consent) by the Secretary of State, and would not necessarily be linked to the holding of a scheduled post; but the schedules had a secondary function as providing for each branch a career-structure covering the whole colonial empire. In accepting membership of a unified branch, officers would become entitled to consideration for advancement in that branch wherever suitable vacancies might occur, and they would also accept a certain limited liability to serve in any colonial territory to which the Secretary of State might from time to time assign them.*

The main purpose of the unification scheme, as has already been shown, was to aid recruitment by offering candidates admission to a corporate Service with a promise of consideration for advancement to any of the scheduled posts for which their qualifications and merits might make them eligible. The results, from the point of view of recruitment, were satisfactory, and the efforts of the Colonial Office between 1930 and 1939 to standardize and where desirable to improve the conditions of employment throughout the Service contributed to the successful establishment of the Colonial Service in the public mind as a body with a high prestige and considerable attraction to adventurous young people with good personal and educational qualifications. This was of great value to the colonial territories, which needed such people in increasing numbers.

The new organization also brought substantial advantages to the serving officers who had been recruited under the old system and now became foundation members of the unified Service. Their eligibility for promotion outside their territories was now written into the constitution instead of being an uncovenanted act of patronage on the part of the Secretary of State. They benefited too from the improvements in salaries, pension arrangements, and general conditions of employment associated with the development of the unification scheme.

At the same time, there were soon hints of troubles to come. There was, to begin with, the question of the schedules of posts. As drawn up, the schedules covered all posts and grades which at the time were actually or normally filled by people not belonging to the population of the territory concerned. Posts already normally filled by locally recruited staff were not included in the schedules. But the composition of the public services in the territories was not static; in some cases it was changing rapidly. Educational progress was gaining increasing

*A list of the branches, with dates of institution, is given in Appendix II.

momentum, and in many territories the line above which recruitment from outside was necessary showed a marked tendency to shift upwards. Clearly this was bound to lead in time to the withdrawal of posts from the schedules, with a consequent reduction in the opportunities open to members of the unified branches. This could be regarded by these members as going back on the prospects which had been held out to them when they were offered their appointments. It was essential to the success of the unified Service to maintain the career-structure, but it was also the policy of the Colonial Office actively to encourage local people to take part in the public services of their countries so far as they were qualified to do so, and there was growing pressure from political leaders and local staffs in the colonies for acceptance of the principle that whenever any suitable local candidates were available they should have preference, irrespective of the claims of outsiders. This was in direct conflict with the Colonial Office view that, in the interests of the colonies, every vacancy should be filled by the best possible candidate without regard to origin.

There was also the question of the position of the relatively small but in some colonies not inconsiderable number of locally domiciled officers who through holding posts which were scheduled had automatically become members of the unified Service or who were subsequently appointed to scheduled posts. Naturally they expected to receive and did receive the same pay and conditions as their expatriate colleagues, but the latters' remuneration had to be fixed with reference to their special needs (such as the cost of maintaining families and educating children at home) and to extraneous factors such as the rates of pay available in comparable careers open to them. The result was to produce an exaggeratedly high differential between the remuneration of local officers in the unified branches and that of other local officers who did not occupy scheduled posts and were paid at rates comparable with those earned in unofficial employment in the territory. This was an obvious source of tension. Moreover, locally domiciled officers, though valuing the status conferred by membership of the unified Service, did not as a rule wish to be transferred outside their home country nor, if they had wished it, could transfers easily be arranged for them. They could, therefore, reasonably expect preference for promotion in their own territories; but this was contrary to the whole conception of unification.

Again, difficulty arose in the borderland between the scheduled posts, normally filled by expatriate staff, and the subordinate posts, exclusively filled by local staff. In this middle range of senior clerical, technical, and skilled artisan posts, expatriate and local officers often served side by side. Ideally their payment should have been uniform at the rate for the job. In practice, any uniform rate sufficient for the expatriate officer would have been much too high for the local officer. In such a colony as Kenya, there were added complications, since the public service included locally-born officers of European and Asian race as well as Africans.

Problems such as these had ultimately to be settled by the Secretary of State, whose decision was final. It was always (and correctly) maintained that the Colonial Office did not attempt to govern the colonies from Downing Street, but in theory the Secretary of State could control the operations of the colonial governments and in practice he did so, in most cases, until the nineteen-thirties. This decade, which saw the birth of the unified Service, also saw the development of a positive policy on the part of the Colonial Office of granting an increasing measure of responsibility to the unofficial members of the colonial Councils. In the more advanced territories it became customary for financial business (which included questions of establishments and remuneration) to be entrusted to a Finance Committee in which unofficials had a majority. In any ordinary matter the views of the unofficials would be overridden only if grave issues affecting the public interest were considered to be involved. Selected unofficials were included in Executive Councils and in a few cases began informally to exercise quasi-ministerial functions. The Colonial Office had always attached the greatest weight to the opinions and advice of the Governors; the Governors were increasingly now obliged, in giving their opinions and advice, to take account of views expressed by the unofficial members of their Councils and the local Press. However, in the pre-war years this did not present a serious difficulty in the territories where most of the members of the unified branches were employed.

At the centre in London, the permanent staff at the Colonial Office had long been accustomed to go their own way, doing what they thought was right for the territories under their charge, with little interference from outside. The Secretary of State was, of course, the ultimate and unquestioned authority; but Secretaries of State and Parliamentary Under-Secretaries came and went, often holding office for no more than a year or two. To some the Colonial Secretaryship was only an episode in a political career. Many had a genuine interest in the work, and a few were spared long enough by the vagaries of the electorate and the Cabinet-makers to be able to exert a real influence on the proceedings of the Department. Even they, however, were all too often obliged to concentrate a disproportionate amount of their attention on some limited aspect of the Office's work—such as the problem of Palestine up to 1948—which happened to be in the political limelight, and to be content to leave the permanent staff to get on with most of the job in its traditional way.

Generally speaking, Parliamentary and public interest in the colonies was only intermittently aroused, usually when some riot, famine, epidemic, or other disaster brought one of the territories into the headlines. The general indifference was in some ways convenient to the Colonial Office, since it enabled much constructive work to be done, quietly and uncontroversially, in building up efficient administrative organizations in the territories. But anything like a forward policy for the development of the resources of the colonies and the advancement of their peoples could clearly not be undertaken without positive assistance from the mother country, and such assistance could not be forthcoming without the active support of Parliament and the British public.

In the nineteen-thirties two major contributions were made towards creating a new climate of opinion. The report, published in 1938, of a comprehensive survey of the tropical African territories, conducted by Lord Hailey, indicated a need for massive financial and technical assistance for these territories. A series of distressing reports on the conditions of the ancient British colonies in the West Indies led to the appointment in 1938 of a Royal Commission under the chairmanship of Lord Moyne to investigate the problems of that area. The Commission's report, rendered in 1939 but not published (except in summary form) until 1945 (Cmd. 6607), revealed a lamentable state of economic and social affairs which could be remedied only by the application to the West Indies of very substantial assistance from outside. These documents provided the chief evidence which made it possible for the Secretary of State, Mr Malcolm MacDonald, to institute the proceedings leading to the passage in 1940 of the first Colonial Development and Welfare Act, under which substantial sums were made available from United Kingdom funds to provide aid to the colonial dependencies.

The adoption of this new positive policy changed the whole background of the Colonial Service. The colonial administrations would not only receive financial help and technical advice in framing and providing for their development programmes, but would need qualified staffs to carry out the programmes. A well-equipped Colonial Service was now a necessary instrument of British colonial policy. The unification scheme had gone some way towards creating such an instrument. Had it gone far enough? Could the Service effectively discharge its new role within the existing administrative framework, based as it was on the principle that the public service of each territory was a distinct entity and that every officer was simply and solely employed and paid by the government of the territory in which he was for the time being serving? Could anything be learned, for example, from the experience of the French who, through the accidents of historical evolution, had built up quite a different system for the administration of their great colonial empire? Such questionings were very much in the minds of the staff of the Colonial Service Division of the Colonial Office, whose business it was to think about them. Other people had other problems to engage their immediate attention.

2

PLANNING FOR PEACE

While the energies of the British government were concentrated on the immediate task of prosecuting the war, the Colonial Office was also heavily engaged in the more congenial work of planning for the future, in the confident hope that, sooner or later, the war would be won and it would become possible to go ahead with the new forward colonial policy. It was accepted as essential to the war effort that the colonies should meanwhile continue as far as possible to be adequately staffed so that they could make their contribution to the common cause. Candidates selected for the Colonial Service were directed to take up their posts, and serving officers were, as a rule, required to carry on with their normal duties even though they would have preferred to volunteer for assignment to the fighting forces. Many of those serving in colonies not directly affected by the war found this restriction irksome, but they were not exempt from making sacrifices. Leave arrangements were disrupted, families separated, journeys fraught with danger. Prolonged periods of work in the tropics without proper holiday, coupled with anxieties about their country and their folks at home, were bound to affect health and morale. The cost of living mounted, and adjustments of pay to meet the increase were seldom as adequate or as promptly conceded as the officers concerned could have wished.

It would be impossible to deal here with all the complexities of the war-time situation of the Colonial Service in all the territories. It will be convenient to concentrate, by way of illustration, on West Africa, where, for various reasons, most of the principal difficulties arose in an acute form. At the beginning of the war, the number of European officers employed in the unified Service as a whole was about 7,000, and about half of these were serving in West Africa. Climatic conditions there were trying; officers often had to leave their wives, and nearly always their children, at home in the United Kingdom; tours of service were extended far beyond their normal length. It was clear that the projected expansion of development and welfare services would call for greatly increased government establishments, and that it would be both politically and economically necessary that these should be staffed predominantly by Africans, who would progressively take over work hitherto done exclusively by Europeans. This process had already begun, and before the end of the war a number of young Africans who were later to achieve great distinction, not only in their own countries but in the international sphere, had been appointed by the Secretary of State to senior posts. African political opinion, which was becoming increasingly vocal, accepted on the whole the necessity of employing expatriate officers but was beginning to grudge the cost which was borne by the local taxpayer, and there was strong pressure from African leaders and the spokesmen of African civil service associations that the principle of equal pay for equal work should be applied. Though it was recognized that an expatriate officer had certain expenses not incurred by his local colleague, and could properly claim compensation for these, it was urged that such differentiation should be restricted to the necessary minimum. But opinions might well differ as to what constituted that necessary minimum.

A constructive attempt to deal with this issue was made by Sir Alan Burns, Governor of the Gold Coast, in 1942. His plan was to draw up a series of new basic scales so contrived that an addition of one-third 'expatriation pay' would give the European officers approximately what they received under the existing scales. The Colonial Office did not like this idea very much, because, in effect, it based the whole pay structure on what it cost to attract European officers to choose service in West Africa in preference to other careers open to them in their own or other countries. To impose on the African colonies an income policy for the public service based not on the standards of the local community but on quite extraneous considerations would be extravagant financially and undesirable socially. Yet the general level of incomes of Africans employed in industry or engaged in agriculture was such that a pay structure based on it would be too low for a mere addition of one-third to bring salaries up to European requirements.

Discussion dragged on rather inconclusively amid the preoccupations of war-time. Meanwhile neither the lot nor the morale of the European officers improved. Owing to the fear of inflation they were not given any cost-of-living bonus. They felt that the Colonial Office was more concerned to placate African opinion for political reasons than to alleviate their grievances. By the beginning of 1944 the Resident Minister in West Africa (Lord Swinton) felt that the position was becoming serious, and at his request the Secretary of State (Mr Oliver Stanley) sent me out to investigate the situation and discuss it with the War Council, which consisted of the Resident Minister and the Governors of the four territories. For two months, while D-Day was being mounted in Europe and the flying bombs were beginning to fall on England, I went about, talking to officials of all ranks and races, civil service associations, and Legislative Councillors. The European associations were naturally most concerned about the inadequacy of their pay and conditions; the African associations pressed for more access to better paid posts and a reduction of the difference between the respective emoluments of Africans and Europeans. I concluded that the most practical solution of the problem lay in abolishing the traditional division of the public services into 'European' and 'non-European' posts and setting up a three-tier system. The top tier would comprise the principal administrative and professional staffs. In practice this tier was and would be mainly staffed by expatriate officers, and its salary scales could be so contrived that basic pay plus expatriation allowance would add up to adequate remuneration for them. The lowest tier would cover posts in which only Africans were ever employed, and salaries for this tier would be fixed at rates appropriate to local conditions and general income levels. In between, comprising the second tier, would be the wide range of posts which might be filled by Africans or Europeans. Since the tendency must be for this range to be taken over entirely by Africans, the salaries should be related to those of the third tier. In so far as Europeans were temporarily required for these posts, pending an adequate supply of African candidates, they should be engaged on contract at *ad hoc* rates sufficient for their needs.

Such a scheme might have worked, but at that period of the war it was difficult to get this sort of general question seriously considered. The Colonial Office and the Governors agreed that as soon as the war was over steps should be taken to hold a formal and comprehensive enquiry and in November 1945 Sir Walter Harragin, Chief Justice of the Gold Coast, was commissioned to carry out this task for the West African territories.

Sir Walter found the Service generally in what he described as a very unhappy state.* Morale had deteriorated considerably even since I was there in the previous year; although some compensation had been given for the rise in the cost of living this was stigmatized as too little and too late. 'It was interesting', wrote Harragin, 'to note that the blame was placed upon the Secretary of State and not the local Government for the failure to redress their grievances earlier.' He produced a very comprehensive report which effectively covered the problems of Service organization so far as West Africa was concerned and proved to be a valuable model for other Commissions which were appointed during the years immediately following the war to examine similar problems in other regions and territories. In considering the rates of remuneration for expatriate officers, Harragin took into account

*Col. No. 209, 1947, *Report of the Commission on the Civil Services of British West Africa 1945–46.*

the current conditions of employment in commerce, industry, and the civil service in the United Kingdom, and also the need of the European in West Africa for regular home leave and assistance in maintaining his family at home. On the question of African remuneration he referred to an interesting observation by one of the witnesses regarding the desirability of creating a middle class in the West African territories and the contribution which the civil service could make towards achieving this. Harragin evidently felt some sympathy with this view, for, while considering that the subordinate clerical grades were not at all badly paid in comparison with their better qualified counterparts in England and in relation to their efficiency—enjoying 'a paradise for the black-coated worker'—he thought that the pay of the superior technical and office staffs should be substantially improved. The fact that such improvement would widen the gap between the financial position of the civil servant and that of his peasant brother should not, in his opinion, be allowed to prevent the adoption of this policy. Any movement towards equalization should take the form of improving the lot of the peasant.

It was not the fault of Sir Walter Harragin or of his scheme that the disillusionment of the European members of the West African services was but little checked by the publication of his report. Political difficulties, especially in the Gold Coast, hampered the improvement of conditions for expatriate officers, who saw various measures turned down or delayed for, as it seemed to them, no good reason. It was not a healthy situation at a time when heroic efforts were needed to recruit new expatriate officers in large numbers to make good war wastage and to provide for the implementation of the development policy.

For the Colonial Office this was not only a West African problem. All the territories had development plans and needed staff. It was not just a matter of finding candidates. It was no use trying to find them unless there was a worth-while Service which they could be invited to join: a Service not only worth-while but seen to be worth-while, not only by the aspiring candidate but by the educational authorities and professional bodies to which he looked for guidance in choosing a career. To remedy the grievances of serving officers was desirable in itself; it was vital to the success of recruitment. There could be no better advertisement than a contented Service, no worse one than a disgruntled Service, especially if discontent was expressed by serving officers in the form of open distrust both of the colonial governments which employed them and of the will or ability of the Secretary of State to support them by standing up either to colonial legislators or to his colleagues in the British government.

Nor could the Service be judged only on the attractions it could

offer at the time. Prospective candidates had to look ahead before com-
mitting themselves. Could they confidently expect to have a career
for the next twenty or thirty years? What were the chances of their
jobs coming to an end prematurely in circumstances in which they
might well be thrown upon the labour market at an unpropitious time?
Given the obvious trend of the colonial territories towards self-government and the prospect that, as education advanced, more local people
would qualify for administrative and professional posts, what assurance
could they be given that their interests and security would be effectively
watched over by the Secretary of State who, after all, was inviting them
to enter the Service under a set of regulations implying a degree of
central control which was likely to become progressively less effectual?

It was clear enough to those in the Colonial Office who were actually
dealing with the affairs of the Colonial Service that these questions
were of crucial importance. The fact that the Service was nominally
unified cut both ways. Unification had been necessary in order to
attract and retain well-qualified staff. But the strength of the chain was
in its weakest link. If the conditions in any territory or group of
territories employing substantial numbers of expatriate officers were
unsatisfactory, the attraction of the whole Service must unavoidably
be diminished. And yet the general policy and practice of the Colonial
Office was firmly based on the principle of treating each territory as
an individual unit managing its affairs in its own way. Coordinated
action, in Service as in other matters, was to be secured by persuasion,
not direction. So long as local responsibility had rested with the
Governors this did not matter a great deal, since the Governors and the
Colonial Office were both parts of the British system and spoke the
same language, even when they argued. But as local responsibility
shifted to local leaders and politicians who approached questions from
a local and not a British point of view, persuasion became more
difficult and direction even less possible.

The problem which confronted the Personnel Division (later called
the Colonial Service Division) of the Colonial Office from the war
years right up to 1956 was how, in the context of these conflicting
pressures and interests, to devise a Service structure which would
incorporate sufficient guarantees of security and stability to maintain
the contentment of serving officers and offer the potential recruit a
reasonably settled career. The efforts to solve this problem are the subject of the present study. Before discussing them, however, it will be
convenient to notice the action taken to organize recruitment and
training.

By 1939 the Colonial Office had built up a well-established and
efficient recruiting machine under the direction of Major Furse, who

had been in the business since his first appointment as an Assistant Private Secretary to the Secretary of State in 1910. At the end of the first world war, in which he served with distinction, Furse was invited to return to the private office to organize the replenishment of the staffs of the colonial territories and the recruitment of the hundreds of new officers whom they needed in an ever-widening range of professional and technical skills. With a small team of his own choosing Furse carried out a miracle of improvisation and laid the foundation of a permanent recruiting organization based on the system of selection. As I have observed above, all this was done technically as part of the Secretary of State's patronage. Furse and his colleagues remained private secretaries without security of tenure or expectation of pension until the position was put right on the introduction of the unification scheme in 1930. Throughout the whole period Furse and his system enjoyed the full confidence of Secretaries of State, colonial Governors, and (after 1930) the Colonial Service Appointments Board.

Furse was determined that the Colonial Office should not be caught unprepared at the end of the second world war as it had been in 1918. 'When the balloons come down for good', he wrote, 'the curtain will go up on a colonial stage set for a new act.' Not only would large numbers of staff be required: quality would be all-important. The pioneer era of colonial administration had passed. The Colonial Service would be operating against a background of criticism and questioning from outside, and of political and social development in the territories themselves. Within the Service itself there was need for greater understanding and cooperation between the different branches—administrative and professional—than had been customary in the past.

These considerations were expounded by Furse in a cogently argued memorandum which he presented to the Secretary of State in February 1943.* His conclusion was that paramount importance should be attached not only to the selection but to the training of recruits for all branches of the Colonial Service in the post-war years. Selection and training should, in fact, be combined in a 'sandwich' operation. As in the past, new recruits would in most cases have preliminary professional training before going overseas on probation. After one or two years of practical work in the field, members of all branches, including officers recruited in the colonies themselves, should be assembled to take together a second course in which the problems of colonial administration and development could be properly studied in the light of the practical experience.

Where should this proposed training take place? Some people had argued for concentrating it at one university, perhaps one of the newer

*Col. No. 198, 1946, *Post-war Training for the Colonial Service.*

foundations, which would thus become the recognized centre for colonial studies. Others (such as Lord Trenchard) advocated the creation of a new Colonial Service Staff College. Furse examined these ideas and gave reasons for rejecting them in favour of a cooperative scheme based on the universities of Oxford, Cambridge, and London, all of which had already taken part in the pre-war training courses for the Colonial Administrative Service.

After consultations in the Colonial Office and with colonial governments and other authorities competent to advise, Furse's plan was accepted in principle, and in March 1944 the Secretary of State (Mr Oliver Stanley) appointed a committee under the chairmanship of the Duke of Devonshire, Parliamentary Under-Secretary of State, to work out the details. The result was the celebrated 'Devonshire' training scheme (it should more justly have been known as the 'Furse' scheme) which made a very notable contribution to the training of the Colonial Service during the following critical years.*

This is a good example of the kind of coordinated action which could hardly have been achieved in the old days when the colonial governments were the only source of funds. What made it possible was the allocation of money under the Colonial Development and Welfare Acts to cover the initial expenses and a substantial proportion of the running costs. The colonial governments were expected, and did not object, to make contributions in respect of the trained officers whom they received. They were not asked to do what they never liked doing, that is to put money into a central fund to be administered by the Colonial Office in the interests of the colonies generally. Thus, without political complications or suggestions of patronage, a central organization of the utmost value to the territories was set up at a cost to the taxpayer which was tiny in relation to the benefits obtained. These benefits were not limited to the actual training given or to the interdepartmental cooperation within the Service which the courses fostered. The presence of the courses and of the officers attending them at three major universities greatly encouraged the pursuit of studies and research relevant to the problems of developing territories and was also an effective means of promoting recruitment and drawing public attention both to the service and to the countries which it served.

Though the fact is often overlooked in calculating the aid given by the British government to the colonies, the provision by the Colonial Office of a highly efficient and experienced recruiting agency, entirely free of charge to the colonial governments, was quite a significant

---

*In addition to the 'Devonshire' courses, the Colonial Office, in conjunction with universities and other academic and professional institutions, built up a widely-ranging series of specialist courses, conferences, and summer schools.

item. When it came to dealing with the post-war rush, the machine was already there, well oiled and prepared for action. It was only a matter of maintaining and developing the established contacts with the principal sources of supply, expanding the staff* to cope with the greater volume of work, and devising special measures for receiving applications and interviewing prospective candidates at certain overseas centres so that people in the fighting services could be considered in anticipation of demobilization.

At the end of the war the vacancies in unified Service grades reported by the colonial governments as needing to be filled amounted to some 2,500. Within two years these were mostly disposed of, but in the meantime many new vacancies had occurred, so that while by the middle of 1947 the Colonial Office had selected nearly 3,000 new candidates, there were still almost 1,000 posts on the books waiting to be filled.† The kinds of officers required were precisely those for whom there was the keenest competition from other public and private employers. Successful recruitment increasingly depended, as time went on, upon the Colonial Office being in a position to give clear and satisfying answers to the questions which candidates were bound to raise. How far this was possible the next chapter will show.

---

*By the spring of 1946 no fewer than 35 permanent or temporary administrative officers were engaged in this work as compared with a regular pre-war strength of 8 or 9.

† Recruitment continued to run at an average rate of some 1,300 a year up to 1958, after which it fell sharply. Education, Medicine, Nursing, Agriculture, Administration, and Engineering were the largest 'customers'.

3

POST-WAR ORGANIZATION

In order to present a connected narrative I have left aside some important developments to which I must now revert. In July 1941, following representations made by the Personnel Division of the Colonial Office, the Secretary of State (Lord Moyne) appointed a departmental committee to consider the post-war organization of the Colonial Service. The committee, under my chairmanship, included those members of the Office who were specially concerned with the subject, together with Sir Alan Burns, a very experienced colonial civil servant who, having recently been Governor of British Honduras, was at the time working in the Office as an Assistant Under-Secretary of State. Shortly after this he was appointed Governor of the Gold Coast.

In an interim report, submitted in October 1941, the committee described the problems created by the conflicting trends in colonial affairs: the tendency to develop local individuality and encourage each territory to work out its own way of life; and the tendency to pool resources so that, acting together, the territories could secure the advantages of collective bargaining and economize on overhead expenses. Another factor was the increasing tendency, in several of the most important colonies, for the public service to become involved in political controversy. This was the consequence of the Crown Colony system, under which executive power was vested in officials, mostly expatriates, while the unofficials had the privilege of criticism without responsibility. Changes in the organization of the Colonial Service could not cure this, but at least the organization should be such as to remove causes of irritation. The unification scheme had, unfortunately, become such a cause. The scheme was based on the schedules of posts which were designated as normally filled by members of the unified branches. This was necessary in order to give content to the scheme and to offer potential recruits the prospect of a career, but it carried the implication that members of the unified branches (*ex hypothesi* persons for the most part alien to the territory in which they served, and looking to the Colonial Office as their headquarters and the Secretary of State as their patron) had a vested interest in the scheduled posts and would thus have a permanent advantage over local officers.

At the same time there was a continuous growth in the number of qualified local candidates who wished to serve their own communities and were not interested in joining a unified Service. The unification scheme was, therefore, according to the committee, in danger of self-stultification.

The committee's conclusion was that the scheme should be revised so as to apply only to those officers who genuinely formed an interchangeable pool. These should be incorporated in a Service with its own system of pay and grading, established (like the Indian Civil Service) by Act of Parliament. The salaries and conditions of employment would be fixed by the Secretary of State and would not be alterable by colonial legislatures but the financial liability of a colonial government in respect of any officer would be limited to the amount provided for his post in the colony's estimates, as approved by the legislature. No posts would be reserved for members of the unified Service, and persons resident in the colonies would not be admitted to membership except in the event of their transfer from their home colony to another, when they would receive the same treatment as other expatriate officers.

It was proposed that the new and genuinely unified Service to which this scheme would apply should be given a distinctive title, such as the Colonial Service (General List). Schedules of posts would disappear and the Service would be made up into separate professional divisions, with uniform graded salary scales in each division. There would be a central pension fund for officers and their dependants. The expenses of running the Service would be met from a general account to which colonial governments would make contributions based on the number of officers of the Service currently in their employment. Under this plan it would, for example, be possible for a poor colony needing, say, a high-powered Director of Agriculture, to be assigned from the General List a suitable officer for whom in the ordinary way it could not have afforded to pay. The colony would contribute the sum normally provided in its estimates for his post and the general fund would make up the difference between the colony's contribution and his General List salary. It was calculated, perhaps optimistically, but on the best information available at the time, that such a scheme could be run at a cost to the United Kingdom Exchequer of no more than £500,000 a year, which could, it was suggested, be provided from Colonial Development and Welfare funds.

These proposals having been formulated at the official level the next stage was informal discussion with Treasury officials. I have often thought that the relationship of the Colonial Office to the Treasury was rather like that of a colonial Governor to the Colonial Office. In his colony the Governor was the supreme authority, wielding un-questioned sway. But when he wanted to do business with the Colonial Office, his opposite number there would not be an officer of his own rank but the Assistant Secretary, or even the Principal, in the department which dealt with his affairs. He was quite entitled, of course, to go to the Permanent Under-Secretary or a Minister, but he would find that, in practice, they had to get the department's advice anyhow. The Treasury had a somewhat similar arrangement, under which a particular officer had the job of dealing with the affairs, in so far as they concerned the Treasury, of each other government office. Thus a matter which had reached a high level in the office of origin might often be considered, at least to begin with, at a lower level in the Treasury. Since most government offices are engaged in running the business of the United Kingdom, their work presumably touches the Treasury more continuously and intimately than did the work of the Colonial Office. Most of the time the Colonial Office went its own way, since it was concerned mainly with activities paid for by the colonial governments, but it had, of course, to consult the Treasury over any matters affecting its own establishment or involving actual or potential expenditure from the Exchequer. A few of the colonies which could not pay their way received grants in aid from the United Kingdom and their finances were, therefore, subject to Treasury control. The Treasury had to be consulted about any general measures affecting all colonies in so far as it was proposed to apply them to territories under their financial control.

The Treasury officers assigned to the desk which dealt with the Colonial Office changed from time to time. In my experience they were always courteous and helpful, but naturally some were more inclined than others to take a real interest in colonial affairs, which often raised questions for which normal 'Treasury practice' did not provide clear answers. In the present case the Treasury officer with whom I negotiated was, as I recollect, not a junior but Mr (afterwards Sir Henry) Wilson Smith. He was most sympathetic and readily agreed that the Colonial Office scheme could be put up to Ministers with Treasury blessing. The Secretary of State (Lord Cranborne, afterwards Marquess of Salisbury) accepted the plan in principle and referred it to his colleagues, who also gave it a fair wind. The Colonial Office was authorized to proceed with the necessary consultations.

These took the form, at this stage, of personal communications to the colonial Governors. They were asked to consult their senior officials but not, for the time being, the unofficial members of their Councils. It was felt that the plan should not be prematurely exposed to political discussion and criticism: that should come when the preliminaries were out of the way and points of doubt cleared up, so that there would be something authoritative and definite to discuss.

Considered from the point of view of rational organization, the proposals received a warm and often enthusiastic response from the Governors. Those Governors especially who were themselves career members of the Colonial Service and presided over territories employing large numbers of expatriate staff fully agreed that some reform along these lines would be essential for meeting the post-war needs of the colonies. At the same time, some of them, in particular those in charge of the more politically advanced territories, felt obliged to point out some serious difficulties. There would, they believed, be strong local objections to introducing any label, such as the 'General List', which applied distinctively to expatriate officers. They urged that any scheme which would command acceptance from political leaders would have to be so framed as to show at least as much concern for developing the opportunities open to local staff as for improving the lot of European officers. Many Governors thought that no plan would inspire general confidence unless it covered the Colonial Office itself as well as the Colonial Service. Some considered that it would be better to think in terms of planning a series of regional Services than to try to maintain a single Colonial Service.

When these replies had been received and collated, the Colonial Office committee went into session again, and, after considering all that the Governors had said, produced a revised scheme. They dropped the idea of a General List, in view of the objections which had been raised to it, and concentrated on formulating standard conditions of service which would be applicable to all expatriate officers serving in any colony. It was felt that, if a sufficient number of colonial governments would agree to apply the standard terms, the need for having something definite and satisfactory to offer to prospective recruits would largely be met. Some governments would undoubtedly not agree, but most of those which recruited substantial numbers of expatriate staff could reasonably be expected to do so. The revised scheme did not solve the problem of the career structure, but it would not prevent the formation of a genuinely unified Service or of regional services if this were found desirable; it was however pointed out that if any regional service were formed it would be essential for it to be provided with an executive authority to manage it on behalf of the participating governments. It was not considered satisfactory to try to manage a regional service from the Colonial Office.

The committee felt that the strong representations of several Governors justified raising once again the question of integrating the Colonial Office staff with the Colonial Service. This idea, as has been seen, went back at least as far as the days of Sir Samuel Wilson, and, although it had been turned down by the Warren Fisher Committee, it had always had its advocates, especially in the Colonial Service and in some political quarters in the United Kingdom. The main argument put forward for having, in the colonial sphere, a system comparable to the Foreign Service, was that this would ensure that the advice given to the Secretary of State would come from civil servants with first-hand experience of the colonies, which would not only be to his advantage but would give confidence to the governments and people in the colonies and help to cement good relations between the colonies and the mother country.

When the committee's suggestions were circulated for comments in the Office, however, they came in for a barrage of criticism. So far as I recollect, apart from members of the Colonial Service who were seconded to the Office and welcomed the proposal, almost the only voice raised in its favour, outside the Colonial Service Division itself, was that of Mr A. B. (afterwards Sir Andrew) Cohen, then one of the Assistant Secretaries. The great weight of opinion in the Office supported the well-known arguments against fusion. Amongst these was the fact that the functions of the Colonial Office staff and the Colonial Service were essentially quite different. The Office existed to advise and assist the Secretary of State in discharging his responsibilities as a Minister in the British Cabinet. For this purpose he needed officers who were aware of current political and parliamentary trends and the climate of public opinion, who were experienced in the British system of government and knew their way about Whitehall; officers who, precisely because of their detachment from the colonies, could deal objectively and impartially with the questions which came up for decision without being influenced by career considerations or tempted to look at their work generally in terms of the few colonies of which any one of them could have had direct experience.

There was clearly some force in this argument, although it was to some extent belied by the undoubted success of dozens of Colonial Service officers who from time to time, while on temporary attachment to the Office, most acceptably filled administrative posts at all levels, from Assistant Principal to Permanent Under-Secretary of State, as well as the chief advisory posts and even on one occasion, the post of principal Private Secretary to the Secretary of State. The risks were almost certainly much exaggerated. But there were also practical difficulties. The great disparity in size between the Office and the Colonial Service made it certain that only a very small proportion of the latter would ever have the chance of serving in London. Selection would present a formidable problem, and there might be a tendency for personal circumstances rather than sheer merit to enter into consideration. So far as the existing members of the Office were concerned, most of them had arranged their way of life on the basis of a career in the Home Civil Service. They could not be expected to welcome a reorganization which would upset their legitimate prospects of advancement in the Office or the Civil Service and oblige them to accept a liability to be permanently posted abroad. Finally, the Treasury objections to such a scheme were unlikely to be less pronounced than in the days of Warren Fisher. In short, whatever might be said in theory for the idea, and whatever Governors and others might urge in its support, there would have been no earthly possibility of its going through unless there had happened to be a Secretary of State and a Permanent Under-Secretary who attached so much importance to it as to be prepared to override the majority view of the Office staff and fight for the scheme at the highest level and to the last ditch. Since there was no prospect of such heroic championship being forthcoming, the committee was obliged to drop this part of the plan.

The Colonial Service Division then endeavoured to bring matters to a head by drafting their latest scheme (with this omission) in the form of a White Paper which, if approved, could be published as a statement of government policy for the Colonial Service. In this draft, taking the Governors' hint, they laid emphasis first on the importance of developing local services in the colonies themselves. They also recognized that it was not possible to impose on colonial legislatures an obligation to provide conditions of employment related to circumstances outside the territory concerned. The legislatures must be free to decide what conditions they thought it proper, in the light of local circumstances, to offer to their public servants. The Secretary of State, for his part, could properly guarantee certain standard minimum terms to officers whom he recruited for the Colonial Service. If the conditions which the local legislature was able to provide fell short of the guaranteed minimum, the Secretary of State could make up the difference to the officer from funds placed at his disposal from the Exchequer. This would make possible what had hitherto been impossible, the equalization of remuneration and prospects throughout the higher ranks of the Colonial Service. It was not thought that in practice the subvention would be called for in any very large number of cases, and the annual cost to the Exchequer was estimated at £600,000.

It will be seen that this scheme was, in essentials, the same as that which the Treasury and Cabinet had approved in principle, though dressed up rather differently so as to fall in with the suggestions that had been made in the consultations. All this process of consideration had, however, of necessity taken time amid the more pressing preoccupations of carrying on the battle for survival, and it was not until the latter part of 1943 that the plan prepared in the Colonial Service Division was ready for submission to Ministers through the Permanent Under-Secretary. Meanwhile the atmosphere had changed considerably. Lord Cranborne had been succeeded as Secretary of State in 1942 by Mr Oliver Stanley, and earlier in the same year Sir George Gater had replaced Sir Cosmo Parkinson as Permanent Under-Secretary. Parkinson was a Colonial Office man who had begun his service in 1909 and became Permanent Under-Secretary in 1937. He was fully conversant with the problems of the Colonial Service and the efforts of the Office staff to solve them. Shortly before the outbreak of war it was announced that he was to transfer to the Dominions Office and that Gater, who was Clerk to the London County Council, would be appointed to the Colonial Office. Gater was, however, needed by Mr Herbert Morrison to organize the war-time Ministry of Home Security, and so in 1940 Parkinson returned to the Colonial Office, and remained in charge until Gater was able to take over in 1942.

Parkinson has left a unique record of his great knowledge of the Office and his devotion to its work in *The Colonial Office from Within* (Faber, 1947). Gater was a very efficient and conscientious administrator but he had no previous knowledge or experience of the Office or of the colonies, or indeed of the civil service. He had the advantage of bringing a fresh mind to bear on their problems, but was very properly cautious about reaching quick conclusions about the complicated and far-reaching issues which came up for decision. Mr Stanley was greatly interested in his Colonial Office work but, according to my impression, was mainly concerned about its political and economic aspects.

In the circumstances, and at that critical period of the war, an early decision about the long-term future of the Colonial Service could hardly be expected; on the other hand, as the war moved into what began to look like its final phase, the question could not indefinitely lie in abeyance. When I went to West Africa, as already recorded, in May 1944, the matter was still unsettled. However, on the day before I returned in July, the Secretary of State held a meeting with his principal officials to discuss the proposals which had been sent up. His conclusion was that the scheme was, in effect, one to subsidize expatriate officers and that as such, whatever its administrative advantages, it was not one for which it would be politically practicable to seek Parliamentary sanction. From the colonial point of view, he considered, such a move would be contrary to the way the tide was running. It was not a time to be taking a step which would be represented as an attempt to tighten central control. To do so would provoke issues of discrimination and invite pressure from colonial legislatures for the British taxpayer to assume the whole burden of paying British officers. All this would be most inopportune. He therefore directed that the proposals should not be pursued.

The Secretary of State's decision was, I need not say, very disappointing to me and my colleagues in the Colonial Service Division, but it was definite and had to be accepted. It may well, indeed, have been inevitable in the circumstances. It is of interest, however, to observe that the decision was based on an estimate of probable reactions if the scheme had gone forward, and not, so far as I am aware, on any actual objections brought forward from outside the Office, either by the colonial Governors or by the Treasury. Indeed, it may fairly be claimed, in the light of historical perspective, that the reasons given for the rejection of the scheme were not necessarily conclusive. Had the will existed to put the scheme into effect, it should not have been difficult to present it to the public in such a way as to forestall political objections, whether from Members of Parliament or from unofficial leaders in the colonies. Admittedly it could have been interpreted by ill-wishers as an 'imperialist' device; but it could with equal or greater force have been presented as a genuine intervention by the British government aimed at providing the territories with the skilled staffs needed for the implementation, for the benefit of the colonial peoples, of the Development and Welfare policy. At a more propitious time the question might have received further consideration and perhaps obtained a different answer. Anyone who was in London in that summer of 1944, when the fate of the allied landing in Normandy hung in the balance and flying bombs might fall anywhere at any moment, will understand that Ministers and senior officials had little time or attention to spare for dealing with complicated long-term problems of no immediate relevance to the war situation. It was something at least to have a decision and to be in a position to go ahead with action, albeit within the existing framework.

The decision, however, can be seen in retrospect to have been the turning point in the story of the Colonial Service. If the scheme had gone through it would have established the principle that the British government accepted responsibility not only for making suitable staffs available to the colonial territories but also for securing suitable terms for the officers employed and, if necessary, providing funds for this purpose. Although the actual proposal was fairly modest, it carried implications which could have been far-reaching. The future history of the Service would have taken a different and in all probability a happier turn. For once the chance of breaking with tradition, carrying the unification policy to its logical conclusion, and creating a properly organized Service had seemed to be within grasp. Now it was back to square one. Yet the problems which the scheme had been designed to solve remained and it was left to the Office to do its best about them.

One of the first necessities was to have literature available for prospective candidates. A pamphlet entitled *His Majesty's Colonial Service—Post-War Opportunities* (R.D.W.6) was rushed into print and issued early in 1945. It opened with a couple of inspirational pages over the facsimile signature of the Secretary of State. 'After the war is over', he said, 'one of our first duties will be to fulfil our promise to guide the sixty million inhabitants of our colonial territories—now at a most critical stage of their history—along the road to self-government within the British Empire.' After describing in general terms the responsibilities and needs of the Colonial Service, he concluded: 'The Colonial Service offers a fine life but not a soft one . . . Those who join it . . . will be entering a disciplined Service . . . no calling can offer more varied opportunities for a career in the public service, and no other profession in peace-time can give scope for greater initiative or responsibility at an early age.'

All this was said in perfect good faith: that is how things seemed to be at the time. Yet, looking back with the knowledge of what was to follow, one must admit that the whole impression created by the pamphlet was one of an ongoing Service offering a permanent career for as far ahead as anyone could foresee. Prospects were held out of promotion to super-scale posts, departmental headships, and Governorships. Though it was not so stated, it was certainly implied that the Service operated under the general supervision, control, and direction of the Secretary of State, which was, of course, technically true. Since no decision had been taken to clarify the position in the light of the changing relationship between the Secretary of State and the colonial governments, there was nothing else that could be said. And since no changes had been made in the pre-war salary scales and conditions of service, it was not possible to do more than circulate the pre-war recruitment memoranda giving these details about the various branches of the Service, with a general statement that certain alterations in the pre-war terms were contemplated and would be announced later. All appointments would then be subject to the new terms, which would be fully explained to candidates when offers of appointment were being made. Naturally no reference could be made in a recruiting document to the widespread unrest in the Service or to the growing distrust felt by its members in many colonies of the local politicians and of the will or power of the Secretary of State to intervene. It was confidently assumed that these symptoms of war malaise would disappear with the coming peace. The interests of the colonies so obviously demanded that their public services should be contented, and that recruits should be attracted to fill the gaps, that whatever reforms were found necessary would surely be willingly conceded.

This was fair enough; but since the Secretary of State's decision had made it impossible to offer standard terms fixed by him, the necessary reforms had to be considered territory by territory, a process which was bound to take time. Most if not all colonial governments had by now added some cost of living allowances to the pre-war salaries but these were at best a temporary palliative and no substitute for a comprehensive revision such as was needed not only to relieve financial hardship but to adapt the structure of the public services to new social and political environments. Accordingly, during the years immediately following the end of the war, most colonial governments took steps in consultation with the Colonial Office to have the situation examined by an authoritative commission, either appointed locally or brought in from outside to report on a particular territory or group of territories. Sir Walter Harragin's commission in West Africa has already been mentioned. Similarly comprehensive enquiries were conducted elsewhere, for example, in East Africa by Sir Maurice Holmes, Mr T. Fitzgerald, and Mr L. G. Corney, and in Northern Rhodesia and Nyasaland by Mr T. Fitzgerald. In the Far East the problem arose in a different form. There it was not a matter of bringing war-time arrangements up to date but one of starting from scratch to reconstitute the public services of the territories which had been in Japanese occupation.

Since the investigating bodies had not only to consider the problems of the territorial administrations on the spot but to advise on the terms required in order to attract and retain the necessary expatriate staffs, they needed guidelines which they looked to the Colonial Office to supply. The Colonial Service Division therefore set about drafting a new statement of policy for the Colonial Service which would supply this need and also, it was hoped, give present and prospective members of the Service confidence in its future. The result of much deliberation and negotiation between Office departments and between the Office and the Treasury was the White Paper Colonial No. 197, *Organization of the Colonial Service*, published in May 1946, on the authority of the Secretary of State, Mr G. H. (afterwards Viscount) Hall.

The first part of the paper sketched the background: the position of the Colonial Service as the sum of the public services of nearly fifty separate administrative units; the fact that the bulk of the civil servants were of local origin; the need for encouraging the staffing of the public services by local people as far as possible; and the fact that for a long time to come many colonies would need qualified staff from the rest of the Empire and more particularly from the United Kingdom. The policy of unification, it was claimed, had proved to be essentially sound, but its application in detail called for review in the light of the developments of the past fifteen years.

The second part of Colonial No. 197 was rather hopefully headed 'A Plan of Action' but there was not really very much in it. The United Kingdom government would help colonial candidates to qualify for posts in their own countries' services, would recruit as necessary in Britain and the Dominions,* would organize and help to pay for training courses, would financially assist colonies to secure expert staff they could not otherwise afford, and would coordinate the distribution of staff so that the available resources were disposed to the best advantage of the colonies as a whole. The colonial legislatures, for their part, would be invited to adjust their service regulations, legislation, and budgetary provision to conform to the general principles of organization which were desirable if the Colonial Service was to function at the highest level of efficiency.

The third part dealt with recruitment and training, and did provide for some positive action. One million pounds would be allocated from Colonial Development and Welfare funds over the ensuing ten years for the purpose of enabling carefully selected colonial candidates to receive professional and vocational training which would qualify them for the higher grades of the Colonial Service. A further million and a half pounds would be provided from the same source and over the same period to finance training schemes for the Service generally, including especially the training courses recommended by the Devonshire Committee to which I have already referred. This committee's report was simultaneously published as a separate White Paper (Colonial No. 198). In summarizing its recommendations in the main paper the government firmly rejected the idea of setting up a special Colonial Service Staff College.

Part four of Colonial No. 197, headed 'Structure of the Colonial Service', contained a list of general principles which it was hoped that

---

*In 1922 Major Furse made an arrangement with the universities in Canada with a view to interesting young Canadians in the idea of joining the Colonial Service and enabling them to be recommended by a Canadian Board for selection without having to come to England. Five years later similar arrangements were made with the universities in Australia and New Zealand. A rather different procedure was adopted in South Africa, where the scheme was operated by the British High Commissioner who, in addition to his diplomatic functions, was in administrative charge of the three British territories in the area (Basutoland, the Bechuanaland Protectorate, and Swaziland). These arrangements, which were confirmed and developed after unification, worked well and thanks to them the Colonial Service at all times included a numerically small but significant element of officers recruited and domiciled in the old Dominions.

the colonial governments would accept as objectives to be aimed at in framing their individual schemes for their public services. Salaries should be fixed in relation to the job and to local income levels, and should, where necessary, be supplemented by expatriation pay, based on the additional expenses incurred by the expatriate officer, especially in tropical climates, the remuneration available in alternative careers in his home country, and the general standard of remuneration and conditions in the Colonial Service. Free quarters should not be provided but where suitable houses were not readily procurable governments should provide quarters, for which officers should pay rent, their salaries being fixed on this assumption. Home leave at regular intervals, with free or at least assisted passages for officers and their families, should be provided for those whose homes were not in the colony in which they were serving. It should be the aim to substitute annual holidays, using air transport, for long 'tours' of service. Changes of station or residence should be avoided as far as possible, and officers should be encouraged to make homes for themselves with a reasonable prospect of permanence.

The poorer colonies, it was stated, should not be at a disadvantage in obtaining fully qualified staff. If a colony, having made the best financial provision it could, was unable to afford the cost of employing an officer whom it needed, it could properly seek assistance under the Colonial Development and Welfare Act as part of a scheme relating to the work or department of the officer concerned. (This was as far as the Office could go in the direction of establishing an equalization fund, but it was not at all an adequate substitute.)

The Secretary of State would continue to control, in the best interests of the colonies, appointments to the higher administrative and professional posts. All branches of the Service would be open to all officers, without distinction of race or domicile, provided that they possessed the specified professional or educational qualifications. Officers would accept the same limited liability to transfer as before, and locally recruited officers who so desired would be given opportunities of transfer but would not be liable to be sent compulsorily outside their home countries. Rigid departmentalism should be avoided, and officers should be placed where their qualifications and experience could best be used. There should be the fullest possible interchange between headquarters and the field, as also between the Colonial Office and the Colonial Service. Suitable professional officers should be given opportunities to undertake administrative work,* and every

---

*E.g. a distinguished officer of the Colonial Medical Service, Sir Selwyn Selwyn-Clarke, was appointed Governor of Seychelles in 1947; such appointments, however, continued to be rare.

effort should be made to encourage the team spirit and the idea that all branches of the Service were partners in the same enterprise.

Finally it was laid down that, in selecting and appointing local candidates to the public service of a colony the Governor should be advised by a Public Service Commission, appointed by him and so composed as to command the confidence of the Service and the public.

Part five of the White Paper dealt with central and regional services. Although no general Colonial Service was being established, there were certain specialized fields in which there was need for central services under central control by the Secretary of State. One group comprised the biological research services, for which teams would be formed with a central directorate, the cost being met from the research allocation under the Colonial Development and Welfare Act. This foreshadowed the creation of the Colonial Research Service to which I shall refer later. The other group covered the land survey, geological survey, and meteorological branches, which would be similarly dealt with. It was also proposed to develop regional arrangements for the pooling of staff by neighbouring colonies where suitable conditions existed.

Next came a section about retirement and pensions. The fact that pensions were provided for by local laws and that there was no general pension scheme for the Colonial Service as such was recognized to involve certain disadvantages but it was concluded that any attempt to impose a uniform system on colonial governments was not practicable. The colonial governments would, however, be asked to review their pension laws so as to conform to certain general principles. These included attaching pensionable status to the officer personally and not (as had been the custom) to the post which he held and a new provision for pensioning an officer before retiring age if the Secretary of State and the Governor considered his retirement to be in the public interest. Proposals were envisaged for a centrally organized widows' and orphans' pensions scheme to cover expatriate officers serving in colonies which had no local scheme.

Another new proposal concerned the creation of a central superannuation scheme on the lines of the Federated Superannuation System for Universities. This was designed to meet the needs of research workers, teachers, engineers, and others who might serve in the colonies for limited periods and pass from and to the employment of other authorities in the course of their careers. Such a system possessed many advantages and it was thought that in time it might be capable of extension to expatriate officers generally.

In the final section of the White Paper, dealing with financial provisions, reference was made to the suggestion that it would be simpler and more convenient for the British government to take over the whole liability for the cost of expatriate officers, thus releasing large funds which the colonies could then devote to development purposes. This idea was rejected as being alien to the whole principle of progressive constitutional development on which the structure and organization of the Colonial Service was based. Such an arrangement, it was said, would be politically retrograde and would create an impassable gulf between the expatriate officers and their colonial colleagues, seriously impairing the spirit of cooperation in a common task which it was so essential to foster.

Taken as a whole, Colonial No. 197 contained nothing that was startling and little that was really new. It was not a very impressive document but it was the best that the Colonial Service Division of the Colonial Office could achieve in the circumstances, since there was no disposition on the part of the Permanent Under-Secretary (Sir George Gater) to advise a radical reconsideration of the policy laid down by Mr Stanley, or on the part of the Secretary of State (Mr Hall) to review his predecessor's decision regarding the structure of the Service. No substitute, therefore, could be offered for the existing unification scheme which on the face of it appeared to be working well. Few could at that time appreciate that that scheme, devised as it was to suit pre-war conditions, was bound to become ineffective and indeed divisive as increasing emphasis was laid on the desirability of building up locally-staffed public services and of allowing local legislators a more decisive voice in the government of their countries.

However, the statement, though consisting so largely of an expression of hopes, the fulfilment of which was contingent on the cooperation of Colonial legislatures, was useful, so far as it went, in the immediate situation. The guidelines which it provided were undoubtedly helpful to those who had the task of reorganizing the public services of the individual colonies in the post-war period, and a fair amount of uniformity in general conditions was in fact secured, by 1948 or so, in most of the territories where expatriate officers were employed in significant numbers. Allowing for variations in local circumstances there was also a broad measure of equality in the salaries provided for these officers, since the salary commissioners naturally took counsel with the Colonial Office, advised in its turn by university appointments boards and by professional institutions, when working out their recommendations.

There remained anomalies. In some of the old West Indian and Atlantic colonies 'imported officers' were still expected by the local legislators to exist on salaries which, unless they possessed private means, often brought them literally to the verge of bankruptcy, and the Secretary of State had no power to do anything about it except to offer the officers concerned transfers elsewhere when he had an opportunity and not to replace them unless by volunteers. But over the Colonial Service as a whole, although in some places pay and conditions of service continued to be a source of discontent, a new phase was developing in which the crucial issue was that of security of tenure.

4

INSECURITY

In 1947, as a result of long and sometimes dramatic negotiations, the British government decided to confer independence on Ceylon, the 'premier colony'. Ceylon, which became a British colony in 1802, had a 'Crown Colony' form of government until 1931, when a new constitution was introduced, giving the island a large measure of internal self-government. Ceylonese Ministers were placed in charge of government departments. A Public Service Commission, advisory to the Governor, was established to deal with appointments, promotions, and discipline.

Although under the 1931 constitution the Secretary of State retained the ultimate responsibility for salaries, pensions, and conditions of service, the Commission (headed by Lord Donoughmore) which devised the constitution had recommended that all officers then in the employment of the Ceylon government whose appointments were subject to the approval of the Secretary of State (which meant in effect all public servants, both European and Ceylonese, except those in the subordinate grades) should be given a continuing option to retire at any time with proportionate pension plus compensation for loss of career. This was based on the view that the constitutional change would involve some loss of prospects (for example the status of official heads of departments would be reduced), and—what was perhaps considered to be more important—that the transfer of executive direction from the Governor to the State Council involved a fundamental alteration in the conditions and understandings on which the officers had agreed to serve. At the time this seemed a natural and reasonable course to adopt. One of the disadvantages of the Crown Colony system was that it created tension between officials and unofficials, and this had become acute in Ceylon. Moreover, as the Colonial Office was organized in 1929, when the decision to adopt the Donoughmore Commission's recommendations was taken, this was treated entirely as a Ceylon matter. There was no unified Colonial Service, and no machinery for ensuring that a question of this kind should be considered as a policy issue affecting the colonies generally.

During the period for which the Donoughmore constitution was in force a number of European and other officers took advantage of the provision for retirement with compensation, but many stayed on, and from time to time others were appointed, as members of the unified Service, to posts in Ceylon for which qualified Ceylonese candidates were not available. The granting of independence after the war meant a much more far-reaching change in the position of public servants in Ceylon than had been effected by the 1931 constitution. Under the latter the Secretary of State—indeed, in the last resort the British Parliament—had remained the final authority, even though in practice the extent to which the British government would exercise its power to override the Ceylon State Council might be doubtful. It could be done, however: for example, since the State Council refused on principle to vote money to provide leave passages for non-Ceylonese officers, the Governor, with the Secretary of State's approval, was accustomed to use his special powers to 'certify' the provision as necessary in the public interest. With independence these special powers would, of course, disappear, and the Ceylon Parliament would be the final authority.

This understandably gave serious concern to the members of the Ceylon public service, especially those who belonged to the unified Colonial Service. They felt that the British government should at least guarantee their pensions and those of their dependants, not because they distrusted the leaders of Ceylon at the time, but because there could be no certainty, once Ceylon had become a sovereign state, that some future Ceylonese government might not stop payment, whether for financial or for political reasons. Naturally this idea found no favour with the British Treasury. As a part of the independence settlement, however, the Ceylon government entered into a formal agreement to continue payment of all due salaries and pensions from Ceylon funds. With this and the continuing right to retire with compensation the officers had to be content. The agreement was one between governments, not between the Ceylon government and its officers. If Ceylon had defaulted it would, strictly speaking, have been the British government and not the officers concerned who would have been the aggrieved party. But in fact Ceylon has honourably discharged its obligations.

In 1948 Ceylon could no longer, as in 1931, be considered as a separate case, apart from the rest of the colonial empire. What was done in Ceylon was bound to set a pattern for other territories which might become independent. The recruitment literature (R.D.W.6, etc.) on the strength of which post-war candidates entered the Colonial Service made it clear that the task of the Service was to guide the territories to self-government. It might have been argued with justice that political advances in the territories were not a departure from but a fulfilment of the understandings on which officers had been recruited and should not be considered as involving loss of career, except for those who might actually become redundant as a result of those changes. But in the light of the Ceylon precedent it would have been difficult in practice to sustain such an argument, nor indeed would it have found much acceptance amongst the staffs concerned. For, although it would be some years (albeit many fewer than most people expected) before any other colony achieved full independence, already the writing was on the wall.

Meanwhile, recruitment for the Colonial Service on the basis of its offering a full and satisfying career was in full swing. No one had any serious doubts about the rightness of this, since there was every indication that the collective needs of the territories for skilled expatriate staffs would continue for a great many years to come, and that any reduction of requirements in one area would be balanced by growing demands in others.* It was plain, however, that the British government would be failing in its duty to the officers recruited under its auspices if it did not make proper provision for their security. This basic issue over which Colonial No. 197 had skated remained to be dealt with. In 1947, therefore, the Colonial Office once again addressed itself to the problem. The Secretary of State was now Mr Arthur Creech Jones, the Labour Party's acknowledged specialist on colonial affairs. Sir George Gater had been succeeded as Permanent Under-Secretary of State by Sir Thomas Lloyd, a man with long experience of the Office and a close knowledge of the Colonial Service. The time was ripe for a re-examination of the situation.

One idea considered in the Colonial Service Division was that, instead of trying to go on with a unified Service covering all the grades in all the colonies, we should aim at building up integrated territorial or regional services. There were four main groups which could be dealt with regionally; East and Central Africa; West Africa; Malaya and the Borneo territories; Fiji and the Western Pacific. The remaining scattered territories would form a fifth group, which would be managed from the Colonial Office. In each of the four regions the governments would be asked to organize interchangeable services, managed jointly and paid on uniform salary scales fixed to suit local conditions. The Secretary of State would act as agent for the groups in recruiting staff as required. This arrangement would apply to posts within the normal time-scales. The Secretary of State would retain control of posts above the time-scales and would fill them (as before) by selecting

*As late as 1955 the Colonial Office was issuing a booklet entitled *A Career in the Overseas Civil Service* by Sir Kenneth Bradley, the preface to which suggested a picture of continuing expansion and development, calling for an undiminished flow of administrators, doctors, engineers, educationists, etc.

suitable officers from the Colonial Service as a whole or by direct recruitment if special qualifications were required. These officers would be regarded as a general inter-colonial Service and would serve under guaranteed terms. In other words, the unified Service would comprise only the higher grades.

Discussion in the Office led to the conclusion that, whatever merits such a plan might have, it was too complicated and did not offer a realistic answer to the problem. It was agreed that the existing unified Service scheme was no longer viable but it was felt that the right course was to keep the idea of a Colonial Service divided into functional branches, without, however, attaching any privileges or status to membership of the branches as such. Instead, attention should be concentrated on the position of officers who had been or would be selected for appointment by the Secretary of State. The weak spot in the existing arrangement was that in fact these officers had a contractual relation only with the colonial government under which they happened to be serving. They had no contractual relation with the Secretary of State, who merely selected them for appointment to the service of a colonial government. True, he told them that they would be subject to the Colonial Regulations, which might be held to imply some moral obligation on his part, but in actual fact this amounted to little more than a promise of protection against unfair dismissal and of consideration of any appeal which an officer who felt aggrieved might put forward through the Governor. The Regulations in themselves gave the Secretary of State no power to remedy grievances. The Colonial Office staff thought that in the circumstances of the time, when the Secretary of State's control of colonial governments and finances was being loosened, officers whom he selected were entitled to something better than this. They should have a contractual relation with the Secretary of State as well as with the colonial governments: he should guarantee their salaries, pensions, etc., while they should accept liability to serve wherever he might send them. They should also be guaranteed a full career or, if this should prove impossible, adequate compensation for loss of career.

It must be emphasized that the proposed guarantee amounted only to an undertaking that, if necessary, the British government would use its constitutional powers to oblige a colonial government to carry out its contractual duty to the officer. It involved no direct undertaking on the part of the British government towards the officer himself. On this basis the Treasury, always, and rightly, concerned to guard against any action which might encourage future territorial governments to default on their obligations, offered no objection to the plan being put to Governors for discussion. Mr Creech Jones, himself a dedicated man, was not very keen about it when it was submitted for his consideration. He felt, perhaps rather naïvely, that young people ought not to be looking for guarantees but should be prepared to go out in a spirit of adventure and take what might come. However, by this time the mood of post-war euphoria had largely evaporated, and candidates were more inclined than before to read the small print as well as the pep stuff. The Secretary of State was persuaded to agree to the reference to Governors, and the proposals were sent to them in a letter from Sir Thomas Lloyd in December 1948.

The Governors generally welcomed the idea of 'de-unification', accompanied by a guarantee of basic terms to officers recruited by the Secretary of State, and the Office staff proceeded to draw up a more detailed plan. The main feature was that the Secretary of State would undertake, on behalf of His Majesty's Government and of the governments of the territories to be named in the schedule, that the terms of service applicable to officers selected by him for posts in the scheduled territories, and not themselves ordinarily resident in the territories to which they were assigned, would not be less favourable than those specified. The specified terms were, broadly, as follows. Salaries would be those approved by the Secretary of State and stated in the offer of appointment. Free passages would be provided for the officer and his wife on appointment and leave. Home leave would be granted at regular intervals, and provision would be made for sick leave and medical attention. Quarters would be made available at a reasonable rent. Pensions would be based on the fraction of 1/600th for every month of service. Retirement would normally be at age 55, but could be at 50 if the officer or the government so desired. In case of retirement on the ground of redundancy, reasonable compensation would be paid by the employing government. No officer would be dismissed or subjected to disciplinary penalties except in accordance with the procedure laid down by the Secretary of State and embodied in the Colonial Regulations.

As will be seen, these were very modest requirements. The Secretary of State could hardly with decency offer less to persons whom he was inviting to join the Service, and in fact all the territories which employed substantial numbers of expatriate officers already provided these or even better terms. Indeed, there was some doubt in the Colonial Office whether the plan went far enough to be really useful, and there was considerable doubt whether it would satisfy the Service. It gave officers protection—in so far as the Secretary of State retained constitutional powers of control—against any variation to their disadvantage of the conditions on which they had been offered and accepted appointment. It was not designed, however, to give them any assurances about prospects or promotions or adjustments to future developments, such as a rise in the cost of living. It was, in short, negative, not constructive. The unified Service as originally constituted largely remained valid, if only the difficulty about career-structure could be overcome. It really needed to be reconstructed rather than scrapped.

With these considerations in mind, some thought was given by the Colonial Service Division of the Colonial Office early in 1950 to another idea based on the principle of keeping the unified Service, but limiting it to the field in which it was really required. The colonies, it was suggested, could be regarded as falling into three categories. There were the large territories, which should and would develop self-contained local public services offering scope for a full career with adequate pay and conditions. These territories should be removed from the unification scheme. The Colonial Office would recruit for them if requested, on an agency basis, but the Secretary of State would incur no responsibility towards the persons so recruited. They would be entirely the servants of the territorial government.

At the other end of the scale were the smaller or less advanced territories which were bound then and for a long time to come to rely upon external recruitment for staffs covering the whole range of government business. In between were territories which could partly provide for their own needs and would increasingly be able to do so, but for the time being needed external help, though they could not offer the prospect of a full career. Would it, then, be practicable to devise a real unified Service which would cover all branches in the lowest tier of colonies, specialized branches in the middle category, and individual posts in the top category? Discussion of these questions by the Office staff led to the conclusion that, while such a scheme might make sense, it would not be comprehensive enough, with the large territories left out, to provide satisfactory career prospects, and that the most useful thing that could be done was to push ahead with the guarantee plan.

One of the Office jokes was about a frustrated correspondent who wrote: 'Somebody at the Colonial Office ought to do something', and the Office was under a good deal of pressure along these rather vague lines. Gone were the days when the Office and the Colonial Service could quietly get on with the job of running the colonies in the light of their own consciences and common sense. Traditionally the Office had not sought publicity or received much public attention, except when something went wrong. It was Mr Malcom MacDonald, when Secretary of State in 1939, who inaugurated a policy of telling the world about the colonies, so as to stimulate public interest and in particular to win support for providing massive financial aid for the Development and Welfare programme. After the war, attacks on colonialism in the United Nations furnished another reason for publicizing British achievements in the dependent territories. In 1949 a successful 'Colonial Month' was staged in London, with an exhibition and numerous Royal and other events. The flags of all the colonies flew proudly from the old Westminster Hospital, proclaimed as the site for the new Colonial Office—which would never be built. There followed a series of 'Colonial Weeks' in cities up and down the country.

By coming thus into the open, the Colonial Office became the target for many and often conflicting pressures; pressures from the right and from the left, from within the colonial empire and from without. There were pressures to administer the colonies more efficiently and pressures to give them more self-government; pressures to give priority to economic development or alternatively to social development; pressures from the Treasury and other government departments; pressures from political leaders in the colonies; pressures from the Colonial Service itself. These last came in the form of petitions and deputations to the Secretary of State, as well as continuous representations made by the Colonial Civil Servants' Association, an organization set up in 1946 by nearly twenty territorial associations to watch their interests in the United Kingdom vis-à-vis Parliament, the Colonial Office, and the public.

Pressures within the Colonial Service arose initially from the situation in West Africa. Not only were the Gold Coast and Nigeria more advanced on the path of constitutional development, but also these territories provided employment for more than a third of the expatriate officers throughout the Empire at the end of the war, as Table I shows. If the Colonial Office were to respond successfully to the demands made upon it, West Africa became a major field of action. The Colonial Service was very Africa-based. Three-quarters of the administrative officers saw service in that continent.

There was a history of tension in the Gold Coast between the civil Service and the politicians. A constitution introduced in 1946 had provided for an elected African majority in the Legislative Council. Following riots which occurred in 1948, an all-African commission was set up to devise a new constitutional arrangement which would satisfy the aspirations of the people. The recommendation of this body that a ministerial form of government should be established was approved in 1950, and in the following year the general election was held which swept Dr Kwame Nkrumah and his party into power.

Meanwhile the state of the civil service in the Gold Coast was far from happy. By 1949 the cost of living had risen so much that the morale of expatriate officers was being seriously affected, and there were threats of large-scale resignations if something was not done to ease their position. Proposals recommended by a local committee and agreed at Whitley Council level were substantially cut down by the Standing Finance Committee. The Senior Civil Servants' Association were naturally dissatisfied with what they considered to be the unreasoned rejection of the proposals, and dismayed by the apparent inability of the government to take firm action. They demanded either effective measures to remedy their grievances or the opportunity to retire with compensation for loss of career or to be transferred to other colonies.

TABLE I. Size of the Colonial Service, 1947 and 1957
Posts under the Secretary of State's control

	1947		1957	
	Total in post	%	Total in post	%
A. *Administrative Posts*				
West Africa	690	38	728	31
East and Central Africa	700	39	1,054	44
Southeast Asia	264	15	350	15
Rest of the Empire	140	8	230	10
	1,794	100	2,362	100
B. *All Other Posts*				
(about)	9,210	(about)	15,640	
Total for the Empire	11,004		18,002	

Source: Staff Lists in each territory (see Appendix III).

At about the same time a local Select Committee recommended that in future expatriate officers should be recruited only on a contract basis. To this the Secretary of State could only reply that, while he was whole-heartedly in support of Africanization, recruitment was already so difficult for West Africa generally and for the Gold Coast in particular that an announcement that appointments would only be made on contract might well be disastrous, and that he could not, therefore, undertake to recruit generally on other than the normal pensionable basis.

While these things were going on in the Gold Coast, the position in Nigeria was not much better. There, too, the senior civil servants were upset by the failure of the legislators to help them in relation to the rising cost of living and were worried not only by their own situation but by the adverse effect which this might have on recruitment, resulting in vacancies remaining unfilled and an increasingly heavy burden being laid on the serving officers.

It was doubtless knowledge of these difficulties which led Lord Tweedsmuir to raise in the House of Lords on 30 November 1949 the question of the Colonial Service—'the steel framework of the administration of Africa'. He drew attention to what he described as an alarming shortage of recruits and to the need to offer a full-time career. Lord Rennell, supporting him, said that the British government must give guarantees that would enable the officers of the Service to live without fear and anxiety for themselves and their families in the future. If this were done, the depleted ranks would rapidly be filled. In reply the Colonial Office Minister of State, Lord Listowel, assured the House that in general recruitment was not running down: the apparent shortage related mostly to recently notified vacancies which there had not yet been time to fill. On the question of security he could not say more than that it was under consideration by the Secretary of State and the colonial governments concerned. And with that Their Lordships had to be content. The Colonial Office was not really as complacent as would appear, but allowance must be made for the difficulty of making any public pronouncement which would not have done as much harm as good to the morale of the Service.

As regards the Gold Coast, much anxious and sympathetic thought was given by both Ministers and officials in the Colonial Office, in consultation with the Governor, Sir Charles Arden-Clarke, to the representations of the civil servants. One thing was clear: the colony needed its expatriate staff, and the aim should be not to encourage them to get out but to make it possible for them to stay. Even if it had been otherwise, transfer to other colonies would not have offered any general solution to their problem. Suitable vacancies could not be made to occur to order, and the interests of the colonies in which vacancies did occur could not be sacrificed to the interests of the Gold Coast service. Experience of the difficulties arising from the termination of the Palestine mandate in 1948 showed the limitations of transfer as a refuge for redundant officers.

On the question of compensation for loss of career, the official view in the Colonial Office was that this should not arise at that stage. The introduction of a ministerial form of government would make some changes in the work of civil servants, but their constitutional position in relation to the government as employer would remain unaltered. The situation was different from that in Ceylon in 1931, since it was now well understood that political changes in the direction of greater local autonomy were to be expected. To concede, therefore, a right to retire with compensation would be, or could be represented to be, an admission of lack of confidence in the willingness of the future African government to give the Service a fair deal, and in the ability of the Secretary of State and the Governor to ensure satisfactory conditions. The effect on recruitment might be grave, since obviously compensation terms could not be offered to new entrants. The repercussions on other colonies had also to be taken into account.

Reasoning along these lines led to the conclusion that the right approach lay in embodying positive safeguards in the constitution of the territory, supplemented by a public statement by the Secretary of State, as recruiting authority, that he would, in the last resort, use his reserved powers to intervene to protect officers whom he had selected for appointment or to secure any necessary improvements in their conditions.

The Gold Coast Legislative Council, for their part, had already agreed that control of the civil service should be removed from the sphere of politics. Under the new constitution a non-political Public Service Commission was established to deal with establishment matters relating to local personnel and to advise on changes in conditions of employment which might become necessary from time to time. The ultimate responsibility of the Secretary of State towards the whole public service, and in particular towards the expatriate officers appointed by his authority, was provided for by vesting the appointment, transfer, dismissal, and discipline of public officers in the Governor 'acting in his discretion'. This meant that the Governor, while consulting Ministers, was not bound to accept their advice but would be subject to the over-riding authority of the Secretary of State. Similarly, no bill or motion affecting the conditions of service of public officers could be introduced in the Legislative Assembly without the consent of the Governor acting in his discretion, and no such bill or measure which in the opinion of the Governor acting in his discretion was prejudicial to the interests of public officers could take effect without the approval of the Secretary of State. These provisions clearly gave public officers all the constitutional safeguards that could reasonably be desired, at any rate on paper. It was not, however, clear what sanctions could in practice be applied if a territorial government should choose to defy them, and they would in any case cease to be effective as soon as a constitutional stage was reached at which the Governor's powers to act otherwise than on the advice of Ministers were removed.

I return to consideration of the general guarantee scheme. The revised plan, drawn up in the light of the Governors' comments on the original draft, was circulated semi-officially by Sir Thomas Lloyd to the Governors in 1950 for further observations, in the hope that it might be brought into force at the beginning of 1951. It soon became clear, however, that this was too optimistic. Several Governors raised points of principle as well as detail, and it took the Colonial Office months to go into all these and re-plan the scheme so as to make it applicable to as many territories as possible. It was the end of 1951 before the final version was ready for submission to Ministers. It had been found possible to include twenty-six colonies in the schedule, subject, in some cases, to minor reservations. Seven colonies were definitely excluded, and some others still doubtful. However, this was considered good enough for going ahead, and armed with the Secretary of State's authority I wrote to the Governors in February 1952 enclosing what was intended to be the final draft. In this version it was stated that the scheme did not apply to officers appointed to posts in their home territory so long as they were serving there, or to officers serving on contract. It was made clear that public servants were employed and paid by the local governments; but in certain cases the Secretary of State selected a candidate and conveyed or authorized an offer of appointment. In such cases (the draft ran) he undertook, on behalf of His Majesty's Government and the government of the territory concerned, that the terms of service specified in the offer would hold good and not be varied to the disadvantage of the officer. This undertaking would apply to officers who had accepted appointments before the date of the statement. Officers selected by the Secretary of State would be liable, as in the past, to be transferred to other colonies on certain conditions, but this liability would not extend to colonies not named in the schedule.

The intention was that the Secretary of State should include this document, when finally agreed, in offers of appointment to posts in scheduled territories. It was not contemplated that the adoption of the scheme should be publicized as a dramatic new departure, but only that the statement should be published in the official gazettes of the scheduled territories for the information of the officers already serving there.

Governors were asked to send their answers by May 1952, so that the scheme could be brought into force during the summer for the main recruiting season. But it was not to be plain sailing. Most of the Governors whose territories were proposed for inclusion in the schedule were agreeable, subject to a few points of detail, but unfortunately these were not the places where the guarantee was really needed. Predictably, in the circumstances described above, the Gold Coast could not be included. The Governor of Nigeria (Sir John Macpherson) felt obliged to advise that the plan had been overtaken by events. In 1951 a constitution had been introduced providing for a Council of Ministers. The Government of Nigeria could not now be committed to anything without reference to the Council. It was very unlikely that the Ministers would accept this scheme, and in any case they would probably require it to be referred to the House of Representatives. The effect of the consequent debates could only be to diminish the confidence of a Service which was already uneasy. To publish the statement with Nigeria omitted would be no less detrimental to morale. What officers needed was an explicit unilateral assurance by HMG that it would continue to look after and guarantee the interests of the expatriate officers no matter what future constitutional changes might take place. Nothing less would now be of any real use.

Malaya and Singapore did not want to be omitted from the Schedule, but the staff associations had raised points which it would take time to examine. Here, too, it was felt that before a commitment was made the Rulers and the Legislative Councils would have to be consulted; a postponement was therefore requested.

Official feeling in the Colonial Office was that, if action were to be further postponed, there was a strong risk that more territories where constitutional developments were in the offing would drop out. Since the territories already excluded or doubtful accounted for a good half of the whole strength of the unified Service, the publication of a scheme from which they were omitted would not do much good and might indeed do harm by stimulating fears where none so far had been felt. The fact was that what had been conceived in 1948 as an uncontroversial administrative operation, mainly confirming existing practice and not involving political issues, had been caught up in the general turmoil of constitutional development. After some months of anxious endeavours in the Office to find some practicable way of meeting the difficulties, the officials were reluctantly forced to the conclusion that there was nothing for it but to abandon the whole idea and rely on writing safeguards on Gold Coast lines into the constitutions of other territories as occasion arose. Advice to this effect was tendered to the Secretary of State and accepted by him. The decision was circulated to the Governors in May 1953. Meanwhile, as the next chapter will show, other ideas were being explored.

The abandonment of the guarantee scheme, on which high hopes had been placed, was another turning point. Looking back, it is natural to wonder whether there may not have been undue delay: whether, if the proposals had been pressed forward more urgently, something might have been achieved before events made it impossible to proceed. It may be so, but this was not a matter which the Colonial Service Division was free to deal with on its own. Within the Office, it involved at every stage references to geographical departments and Advisers, all busy people with many other claims on their attention. Changes of Ministers called for fresh explanations and submissions. When the Office had agreed on proposals they had to be referred to some forty overseas Governors, all of whom needed time for consideration and reply, and many of whom raised points demanding thought and further exchanges of correspondence. Revised proposals would then have to go through a second round of the same procedure, and by then circumstances would have altered. It was by no means a quick or easy matter to get this kind of general question settled in the colonial Empire of the nineteen-fifties. And all this had to be sandwiched in, as best could be done, with the heavy day-to-day work of administration which could not be neglected.

It is also legitimate to wonder whether, if things had gone forward more quickly and the scheme had been put through, it could really have made a great deal of difference. It was not a total loss, as it was. The formulation of the minimum terms which the Secretary of State considered proper for expatriate officers did induce some colonies which had not previously done so to bring their terms up to this standard. More progress might have been made along these lines if the terms had been officially published as applicable to the Service generally. Would the new ministerial governments have felt themselves morally bound by guarantees entered into by the colonial regimes? It is a hypothetical question. Given the unforeseen rapidity of constitutional change in the major colonies at this period, it is probable that no device could have succeeded for very long in preserving the anomaly of a Service whose members were entirely the paid servants of the territorial governments, but were for ever looking over their shoulder to the Secretary of State as their real master. If anything was to be done, it would have to be along quite different lines.

5

SCHEME FOR A BRITISH OVERSEAS SERVICE

In following the guarantee scheme through to its demise I have left some threads of my story to be picked up. Sir Ralph Furse had retired in 1948. From 1910 onwards he had been chiefly and personally responsible for the recruitment and training of the higher grades in all branches of the Colonial Service. His imagination, energy, and flair had created a system of selection which was universally and justly admired. He has been called the 'father' of the Service, and the title is not undeserved.

When Furse and his colleagues were 'established' as an Appointments Department in 1930, it was natural that they should continue as a team, doing the specialized work in which they were expert. As time went on, some of the original members dropped out, for one reason or another, and in the post-war expansion of the department other members of the regular staff were posted in and out, as with any other part of the Office. There was therefore less reason than in the past for preserving the arrangement whereby recruitment was dealt with by one set of people and promotions and transfers by another. The effect of this was that the knowledge of officers appointed to the Service gained by the recruiting staff was liable to be wasted, since that staff had no concern with the later careers of the persons whom they had selected. Yet one of the main functions of the Colonial Service Division was to advise on the selection of candidates within the Service for the scores of vacancies continually cropping up in all branches and at all levels in the various territories. In order to remedy this weakness in the organization, the work of the Division was rearranged in 1949 so as to provide for two 'subject' departments dealing respectively with general recruitment and training, and with general conditions of service; and three 'staffing' departments, dealing both with the selection and with the posting, transfer, and promotion of officers throughout their careers in the various branches of the Service.

In 1948 the Secretary of State (Mr Creech Jones) appointed a small committee under the chairmanship of Sir Thomas Lloyd to consider and advise on any changes that ought to be made in the organization of the Colonial Office in the light of its existing and probable future functions. That part of the committee's report which is of interest in the present connection concerned the question of amalgamating the administrative staffs of the Colonial Office and the Colonial Service into a joint service. The committee observed that this was not a new idea, and that there were warm advocates in both services for and against amalgamation. They did not rule it out as a future possibility, but felt that it could not be a practical proposition until there was a closer balance in numbers between the British members of the Colonial Service and the staff of the Office, and until the work of the former should become principally advisory and technical rather than that of direct administration. As it was, the position differed greatly from that of the Foreign Office and Foreign Service, where fusion had taken place. The committee therefore firmly advised against amalgamation, while making some suggestions for continuing and extending the existing arrangements for interchange on secondment between the two services and for encouraging them to regard themselves as part of one team, with the same interests and the same ends. This view was accepted by the Secretary of State.

Another important event of the same period was the creation, with effect from 1 January 1949, of the last of the branches of the unified Service, the Colonial Research Service. It introduced a new pattern. It was described by the Secretary of State (Mr Creech Jones) in an official despatch to colonial governments as 'a novelty in Colonial Service organization. In the field of research, the scheme carries the principle of unification to its logical conclusion . . . I think that, if this scheme is successfully established, it may point the way for a new future form of organization for the scientific branches of the Colonial Service at any rate, and possibly in time for all staffs who have to be recruited from outside the colonies for posts demanding special experience or qualifications not possessed by local candidates. We may thus be led towards a solution of the problem of applying the principle of unification where it is needed without also imposing it upon locally-recruited staff for whom it has little or no relevance.' It was a reasonable hope: but it was not to be fulfilled.

The Research Service differed from other branches in that its members were often engaged in work which was not part of the regular activities of a colonial government but was in furtherance of a project for which the colony concerned happened to be the most suitable location, and they were paid from the funds made available for the project, whether provided by the territorial governments, the British government (under the special allocation of Colonial Development and Welfare money for research), or, as was most usual, a combination of both. Moreover, research workers were not normally seeking a career in the Colonial Service as such. Their work in the colonies was part of a career which might well involve at different times employment under other governments, academic institutions, or industrial organizations.

To meet these special requirements, the Colonial Research Service was at the outset provided with a basic set of salary scales analogous to those of the Home Scientific Civil Service and those laid down for medical workers by the Medical Research Council. To these basic salaries were added overseas research allowances fixed on a regional arrangement to bring the salaries up to the level of comparable posts in the public services of the territories. There were three rates of allowances: one for workers with medical qualifications, one for those with veterinary qualifications, and one for the rest. Officers entered the scales at points determined by their training and experience and not by reference to the job actually held. (It may be remarked here that this system of basing salaries on home civil service rates did not work out satisfactorily and in 1955 new consolidated rates were drawn up.)

The normal colonial governments' pension schemes, framed for officers making their career in the Colonial Service, clearly did not fit the case of research workers. To meet their needs, and those of others, teachers, engineers, and specialists of various kinds, who might likewise pass in and out of the Colonial Service from and to other forms of employment, the Colonial Office devised and brought into operation in 1951 a Colonial Service Superannuation Scheme analogous to that in force for British universities, under which, in return for contributions paid in by the officer and his employer during service, various optional benefits would be available for the officer and his dependants. It was thought that the general adoption of this scheme for new entrants to the Colonial Service, if this should prove practicable, might go a long way towards removing one of the chief difficulties which colonial governments felt in employing expatriate officers, namely the prospect of building up enormous pension bills to be met by the taxpayers of the distant future, when the officers now at the beginning of their service would be coming to retirement.

While the Colonial Research Service organization thus had several features which the Colonial Service Division would have liked to see applied to the Service generally, the members of this branch were no more than those of any other branch in the employment of the British government, the Colonial Office, or any central authority. Like other members of the Colonial Service, they were constitutionally the servants and employees of the territorial governments. They did not in any real sense form a pool of workers at the disposal of the Secretary of State, though between 1950 and 1953 three very small pools were in fact established in the fields of entomology, plant pathology, and soil science, mainly to enable short-term investigations to be carried out, especially in smaller territories whose establishments did not include the necessary specialists.

When it became clear towards the end of 1952 that the guarantee scheme was likely to break down, and could be of only limited value if it should go through, much thought was given by the Colonial Office staff to the possibility of a new approach to the problem of Colonial Service organization. Effort had so far been directed, not very successfully, to devising some workable scheme consistent with the notion of a Service which was under the general authority and supervision of the Secretary of State but whose members were the employees of territorial governments from which the control of the Secretary of State was being progressively withdrawn. It was important, of course, to provide safeguards for the existing staffs; but it was no less important to look to the future. The traditional framework would obviously become less and less suitable as time went on. What was needed was a framework which would stand up to any constitutional changes and within which the territories could be supplied with the staffs which they would still require from outside.

There was talk about this time of a 'planned withdrawal' from the Gold Coast. In a memorandum which I wrote early in 1952 I observed that under existing arrangements officers who did not want to stay there could only be offered the opportunity of transfer to other colonies, on the off-chance that suitable vacancies could be found, or of retirement with compensation, in which event their experience and ability would be lost to the Service. I painted a depressing picture of the future of the Colonial Service as a series of transfers of officers from one untenable post to another slightly more tenable, until in the end the Administrator of Tristan da Cunha would remain as the sole inheritor of past glories; in short a kind of 'tontine'. What, I suggested, the occasion demanded was the creation of a parent body from which officers could be hired out to overseas governments on request and to which officers could revert when their particular assignments came to an end. This would have to be a British body, maintained and paid for by the British government.

The argument pointed to the need for setting up what was provisionally described as a British Overseas Service, the members of which would be British civil servants, paid on scales analogous to those of the Home Civil Service, with the appropriate overseas allowances when serving abroad. They would be liable to serve wherever the Secretary of State should direct, and would be made available to overseas governments at the latters' request. While seconded overseas they would receive the salary and allowances of their rank in the British service, or the emoluments of the local post, whichever was the greater. The

British government would recover from the borrowing government the officer's British rate of pay and allowances, plus a pension contribution. Candidates would be recruited directly into the Service by the British government, but in the initial stages transfer to it could be offered to officers in the Gold Coast or perhaps even to members of the Colonial Service generally.

Consideration in the Office brought to light the difficulties inherent in any such scheme, notably the difficulty of deciding how many people could safely be recruited into the new Service in the absence of any clear means of forecasting what the future demand of overseas territories for British staffs was likely to be. The question was, how far such difficulties, real as they were, should weigh against the urgent necessity of taking some positive action if the Colonial Service was not to disintegrate within the next few years. It was not only inside the Colonial Office that ideas were germinating. In March 1952 Mr A. D. Dodds-Parker, MP, and Lord Tweedsmuir pressed for the creation of a 'Commonwealth Service'. In May Sir John Sargent wrote to the *Manchester Guardian* urging the need for some kind of new Service to provide experts for developing countries. At the ministerial level, the Minister of State (Mr A. T. Lennox-Boyd, afterwards Viscount Boyd) and the Secretary of State (Mr Oliver Lyttelton, afterwards Viscount Chandos) were attracted by the idea of creating a British Overseas Service and thought that it should be pursued if it could be shown that it would meet a demand.

With this encouragement, the Office staff began informal consultations with the Foreign and Commonwealth Relations Offices, both of which, it was thought, would be interested, and with a number of senior colonial Governors. The Foreign Office indicated that such a Service as had been proposed might well be of value in providing specialists asked for by developing countries outside the Commonwealth, while the Commonwealth Relations Office considered that it might help in providing experts for work under the Colombo Plan. The reactions of the Governors were mixed. There was general support for the plan as a means of setting up a pool of staff for meeting future requirements, but several of them felt that it would not really help in solving the problem of the existing staffs; indeed one Governor thought that the adoption of the scheme might do more harm than good to morale. Other comments made were: that the real problem concerned not the specialists but the administrative officers, and the only satisfactory solution for them would be integration with the Colonial Office; that the scheme should cover all serving expatriate officers with over ten years' service and not within five years of retiring age; and that the really important thing was that the British government should accept full liability for the pensions of existing officers, in return for pension contributions to be paid by the employing governments. One Governor gave the opinion that the right policy was not to set up a British service but to help the territorial governments to establish properly organized and integrated civil services of their own; this solution, however, could apply only to the larger territories.

Support for the idea of a British Overseas Service in the field of medicine came from the Secretary of State's Chief Medical Adviser, Sir Eric Pridie. In 1949 there had been some discussion of the possibility of forming a register of doctors willing to serve overseas. A committee was set up in conjunction with the Ministry of Health, but it was found that there were many difficulties and that on the whole better results were obtained by normal recruitment. Since then, however, the position had altered considerably, and some new approach was urgently needed.

In the light of these preliminary enquiries a working party was set up in 1953 to go more fully into the proposal. Representatives of the Foreign Office, the Commonwealth Relations Office, the Ministry of Labour and National Service, and, later, of the Treasury, were invited to join in the discussions, which now took place against the background of the decision to abandon the guarantee scheme for existing officers of the Colonial Service. The Colonial Office was, in fact, trying to solve two problems, which were distinct though closely related to each other. The first was the problem of keeping the Colonial Service in being and in good heart. It was needed as much as ever by the territories which it served. Its members were in the full flood of work, and the great majority of them wanted nothing better than to carry on with the job for which they had been recruited and to which they were devoted. They were by no means unsympathetic to political developments in the colonies and were quite ready to work in partnership with local ministers and officials. All they asked, very reasonably, was that they should be able to feel that their services were welcomed, and that they were not regarded as intruders or treated as pawns in the local political game; that they should be given fair conditions of employment; and that their salaries and pensions should be firmly guaranteed irrespective of any constitutional changes that might take place in the future.

If these needs could be satisfied, the Colonial Office could feel that the colonies would have the experienced staffs necessary to see them through the transitional stage to independence which, even then, was assumed to be a very long way ahead. In Ceylon, after all, the intermediate stage had lasted for seventeen years, and Ceylon in 1931 was in many ways more advanced in its social progress than the African colonies were in 1953. But 1953 was not 1931. The whole climate had changed. The constitutional experts could strive as they might to devise for each colony an acceptable half-way house on the road to independence, but it took only a very few years to discover that there was no such thing. Even so, it was hardly thinkable in 1953 that within fifteen years thirty-one British colonies would have become independent sovereign States or amalgamated with other independent countries. For the time being the problem was seen as one to be dealt with in circumstances in which the ultimate constitutional power would remain with the British government, however great the degree of autonomy conferred upon a territorial government in respect of its domestic affairs.

Things had moved far enough, however, for it to be necessary to look ahead to the possibility of some at least of the larger territories achieving full independence, if not (as was then thought) in the immediate future, at any rate within the twenty or thirty years of the official lifetime of junior members of the Service and those who were currently being recruited. It was reasonable to assume that even these territories would still need some outside help in staffing for an indefinite time and that it would be in the interests both of the territories and of the United Kingdom that suitable British staffs should be available to provide that help.

Clearly, both problems could have been solved at one stroke if it had been possible to do what most officers of the Colonial Service would have liked, namely to establish a British Overseas Service, to offer all existing members of the Colonial Service the option of transferring to it, and to recruit for it alone thenceforward. Enough has been said already to show that, whatever the attractions of such an idea, it was not practically possible. It would never have been feasible to obtain ministerial, Parliamentary, and Treasury approval for such an open-ended commitment as a scheme of this kind must involve if the fifteen thousand or more officers already serving and those yet to be recruited were to be included. The Colonial Office was forced to the conclusion that, if a new Service could be brought into being, it would have to be designed strictly with an eye to the long-term needs of the territories and not as a cure for the ills of the existing Colonial Service.

Yet, if drastic surgical measures were not practicable, there were, it was felt, ways in which something might be done to give relief. One action which in itself would have transformed the whole atmosphere would have been the concession of a firm British guarantee of pensions for Colonial Service officers and their dependants. This was continually being pressed upon the Colonial Office, especially from Nigeria; but the Treasury was adamant in refusing to commit the British taxpayer to meet obligations which belonged entirely to the territorial governments, no matter what constitutional changes might ensue. As far back as 1950 Mr James Griffiths, when Secretary of State, had had to parry a parliamentary question on the subject by saying that he could not envisage a situation in which the pensions of colonial civil servants would not be secure; he therefore saw no reason whatever for anxiety on this point.* No more than this could be said in 1953. The Treasury view was justified by the fact that there was no real doubt that in the long run (but who knew after what argument, delay, and hardship?) the United Kingdom government would come to the rescue of British pensioners if a territorial government should default on their pensions; but the mood of the Service was distrustful of tacit assumptions that it would be all right on the night.

Another line which the Secretary of State, Mr Oliver Lyttelton, would much have liked to pursue was the grant of some assistance to British Colonial Service officers towards the cost of educating their children. Most of these officers had no practical alternative to sending their children to fee-paying boarding schools at home; the holidays also had to be looked after, and this might involve providing a home base for the officer's wife. These heavy costs were in fact among the main reasons for maintaining the substantial difference between the pay of an expatriate and that of a locally resident officer, which was a bone of contention with colonial politicians.

There had been in existence since 1931 a charitable Trust, established by the generosity of H. H. Rajah Brooke of Sarawak, the income of which was available for making grants to assist European higher civil servants in the colonies, or their widows, in the education of their children. In practice the Trustees were able to help serving officers only in exceptional cases of hardship, since the income was all needed to assist widows and officers who had had to retire prematurely on small pensions for health reasons. The suggestion now made by the Colonial Office staff was that the United Kingdom government should make a substantial addition to the income of the Trust, so that the Trustees could greatly enlarge the scope of their assistance and bring into its range serving officers who, because of their family commitments, were finding it difficult to make ends meet. Such a practical gesture of good-will would, it was thought, help to put heart into the Service by showing that Her Majesty's Government appreciated the situation of its members and was alive to their interests.

Here again, however, the Treasury felt obliged to take a negative attitude. It was not only a matter of finding the money; there was the

*Hansard, House of Commons, 15 December 1950.

question of a precedent which might affect other services. But the main objection was that the proposal involved subsidizing not so much the officers as the territorial governments. It was entirely their responsibility to pay their officers a proper wage, and they should not, in the view of the Treasury, be encouraged to shirk that responsibility.

It is not far from the truth to say that, in that autumn of 1953, the Colonial Office staff was rather desperately trying to find solutions to the problems which pressed upon it. The Office was not alone in realizing that there were problems or in producing ideas. In the September issue of the *National and English Review* Mr (afterwards Sir) Bernard Braine, MP, wrote an article arguing strongly the need for 'a broadly based Commonwealth Service, open to all Her Majesty's subjects, trained to cope with the administrative and technical requirements of this changing age, and offering a secure life-long opportunity for service to Europeans, Asians and Africans alike'. On 7 and 8 September *The Times* (a paper which was always in my experience well-informed and sympathetic in its approach to Colonial Service problems) carried on its leader pages two articles 'from a Special Correspondent' headed 'A Commonwealth Civil Service?' The author pointed out that something was needed to bridge the gap between colonial status and independence. It could not be a continuance of the existing Colonial Service, but the Colonial Service need not be Britain's last word. A new type of service was required, with recruitment, salaries, rank, security, and pension guaranteed by the Mother Country, either acting singly or together with a consortium of other Commonwealth governments. The Service must be conceived, developed, and supported in London. Financial responsibility could be reduced by enlisting the cooperation of the Dominions, but in any case the cost would be trivial compared with the losses which the existence of the new service might prevent.

Some letters to the Editor followed these articles. Mr Gordon Walker doubted the possibility of setting up a new service, but pointed to the need for some instrument of Commonwealth cooperation rather on the lines of the future Commonwealth Secretariat. Lord Birdwood wrote urging the formation of an international pool of experts. Mr W. L. Dale, who was at one time a member of the Colonial Office's legal staff and was then attached to the government of Libya, wrote from there strongly supporting the idea of a centrally recruited and guaranteed service to supply the developing countries with first class officials able to carry out their duties conscientiously and with dignity. Sir Angus Gillan also supported the idea and suggested that a beginning might be made with the excellent officers who were then leaving the Sudan. Sir John Sargent thought that there should be a British service of 'experts for export', sponsored but not controlled by the government.

From within the colonies themselves, the chief pressure now came from Nigeria. The Gold Coast had passed the point of no return, and a constitution giving the country a status just short of independence was about to come into force. The expatriate officers, who comprised at least three quarters of the colony's administrative and professional staff, had been given the right to retire, if they so wished, with compensation, but they had also been offered certain inducements to stay on, at any rate for a time, and many of them were content for the present to do so. The position in Nigeria was much more difficult. The public services were much larger, and contained an even greater proportion of Europeans in the administrative and professional grades; indeed, Nigeria was by far the largest customer for all branches of the unified Service. Over much of this huge country, especially the northern part, the Colonial Service was carrying on its traditional work and asked nothing better than to be allowed to do so, conscious that the country was in no position as yet to staff an efficient administration from its own resources. The political leaders, however, particularly those in the Eastern and Western Regions, that is to say the southern part of the country, were anxious to press forward to self-government. They were, not unnaturally, resentful of the fact that British officials were the real rulers of the country and, although there was nothing personal in their feelings, their public utterances were not always such as to win the officers' confidence in their goodwill. The consequent mood of the Service was illustrated by the proceedings of a conference of District Officers held at Onitsha in July 1953. After setting forth the difficulties of the situation, the conference concluded that the only completely satisfactory solution would be the establishment of a general Colonial Service, employed by Her Majesty's Government and seconded to colonies with guaranteed pay and conditions.

While Nigeria was at the moment in the foreground, much the same kind of unease was developing in the other main fields in which the Colonial Service operated—Malaya and East and Central Africa. It was becoming publicly known that the Colonial Service was, in the words of one very distinguished administrator,* 'in the doldrums'. The continuing need of the colonies for staff, and the extent to which the reputation of the Service as a career had sunk, are illustrated by the fact that in the recruiting season of 1953 the colonies collectively asked for over 200 administrative officers and by the end of October only half the vacancies had been filled.

Against this background, Mr Lyttelton, who had the interests of the

*Sir Gerald Templer, then High Commissioner in Malaya.

Colonial Service very much at heart, directed the Office to prepare a comprehensive plan as a basis for consideration by Ministers, in the hope that the difficulties which had been felt might be overcome and something practical and constructive might emerge. The Office staff accordingly set out to produce a programme with a three-fold objective: to make it easy, politically and financially, for territorial governments to employ British staff; to make it easy for experienced British officers to stay on for as long as they were wanted; and to offer new recruits a satisfactory prospect of a career.

So far as serving officers were concerned, further consideration only confirmed the view that it was useless to consider transferring them wholesale into some new type of service. The financial, political, and administrative difficulties in the way of Her Majesty's Government assuming full responsibility for so large a number were too formidable. No new device could, in itself, create more opportunities for enabling officers redundant in one territory to find employment in another, or increase the willingness of the Secretary of State to give officers the advantage of whatever opportunities there might be. What Her Majesty's Government could do would be to ensure, in any negotiations for constitutional advance in any territory, that the territorial government should enter into a binding agreement to fulfil its contractual obligations towards its officials and to pay adequate compensation to those whom it did not wish to retain or who did not wish to stay. In the particular matter of pensions for officers and their widows or orphans, the Colonial Office still felt, in spite of the objections raised by the Treasury, that Her Majesty's Government should specifically associate itself with the guarantee to be given by the territorial government. This, it was considered, more than any other action, would allay the fears of serving officers and make them content to carry on with their work for so long as they were needed. It would remove the temptation to take the 'golden handshake' while it was available, rather than trust to the goodwill of some future independent government.

The Colonial Office also still felt that the proposal for an educational trust fund should be pursued. Whatever the theoretical objections, the Office maintained that this would provide a simple, effective, and relatively inexpensive means of giving encouragement to the Service, of helping officers who were in real need, and of reducing tension between expatriate staffs and local politicians.

Looking then to the future, and taking into consideration the various ideas which had been put forward, the Colonial Office staff again urged the need for setting up a new British Overseas Service. This was not offered as a device for solving the problem of the existing Service. There might indeed be opportunities of offering selected members of the old Service a transfer to the new one but this would depend on the needs of the new Service for people with particular qualifications or experience, not on the needs of officers to be found jobs. The new Service, as conceived in the Colonial Office, with the help of the other departments represented in the discussions, would be strictly limited in numbers—an establishment ceiling of 5,000 at the start was tentatively suggested—and membership would be confined to people for whom there was a reasonable prospect of employment in one or other of the developing countries for a considerable time to come. The Service would be built up gradually, in response to requests received from overseas governments. The practical mark of membership would be participation in a superannuation scheme managed by the British government. This scheme would be financed by contributions paid by the members and the employing governments, or possibly, the British government might make itself responsible for the employer's contribution, which would be a help to the governments of the developing countries and would obviate the necessity of establishing an actual fund.

The superannuation scheme would, it was suggested, provide for a lump sum gratuity for short-term employees, and a pension plus lump sum for those who served for a minimum period such as ten years and had to retire on account of age, ill-health, or suitable employment not being available. Officers retiring voluntarily before age 50 would get their money back with interest. Pensions would be provided for dependants. Arrangements would be made for preservation of pension rights on transfer from or to other approved employment.

The Service would be run by a special Commission, and officers would agree to serve wherever the Commission might send them. The government or other authority to which an officer was assigned would be asked to give twelve months' notice of its wish to terminate the assignment; that is, it would be liable for its agreed out-goings in respect of the officer for up to a year (including any earned leave) from the date of notice if the officer could not in the meantime be found other employment. At the end of the year, if the officer was still unposted but wished to continue in the Service and had a reasonable prospect of being given another post, he would be placed on the home establishment and do any suitable work which the Commission might direct him to do while thus *en disponabilité*. If at the end of a further specified period, such as six months, the Commission could see no real chance of finding him another regular job, he would retire with such compensation as the superannuation scheme should provide for his particular case.

Such, then, was the package deal which the Colonial Office staff had worked out, by the end of 1953, for the Colonial Service: a pension guarantee for existing members and an educational trust fund to help them with their family expenses; and a new Service for the future, the members of which would be in the employment of the British government and assigned to work under overseas governments only at the request of those governments and on terms fixed and approved by the British government.

6

HMOCS

The package deal, when it arrived on the desks of the higher officials of the Treasury, seems to have caused a certain amount of consternation. The Treasury had indeed been represented at the preliminary discussions about the proposed British Overseas Service, but it was one thing to discuss and another to put up a definite recommendation to Ministers. The Treasury men recognized and sympathized with the difficulties of the Colonial Office but they were far from being convinced that the kind of commitments into which the Colonial Office wished Her Majesty's Government to enter were essential to a solution of the problems. They made it clear that there would have to be a lot more consideration before they could advise the Chancellor of the Exchequer.

The Treasury reactions came at the beginning of 1954, just as the Secretary of State, Mr Lyttelton, was going off to Nigeria to preside over a conference for drawing up the federal constitution of the country which it was aimed to introduce in 1956. Reluctantly he agreed that ministerial consideration of the Colonial Office proposals would have to await his return; meanwhile discussions should proceed at the official level.

In spite of what the Colonial Office had represented, the Treasury were doubtful of the validity of arguments based on a falling-off of recruitment or the alleged danger of mass resignations. They observed that recruitment for India had gone forward satisfactorily long after it had become clear that independence was a definite prospect. Experience showed that, on the whole, people who had chosen a career in the public service did so with the intention of sticking to their jobs, and did in fact stick to their jobs. The Colonial Service was not alone in having recruitment problems; in a period of full employment at home all public services were finding it more difficult to attract sufficient recruits. If existing methods needed to be supplemented, this might be done by helping territorial governments to recruit staff on their own account, or by lending them some home civil servants.

The Colonial Office answer to this was that the Indian parallel was by no means exact, if only because the Indian Civil Service had been comparatively well paid and, unlike the Colonial Service, had been under the protection of an Act of Parliament. It had been authoritatively stated by a high official in Nigeria that 70 per cent of the British officers there would be willing to sacrifice their pensions if they could get other jobs. This was perhaps an overstatement but such talk could not fail to prejudice recruitment for Nigeria itself and for the Colonial Service generally. Secondment of home civil servants could not possibly be on a scale that would make a significant contribution to the staff needs of the territories.

After some preliminary skirmishes along these lines, a formal meeting was convened by the Permanent Secretary of the Treasury and Head of the Civil Service, Sir Edward (afterwards Lord) Bridges, on 15 January 1954, with a view to considering what advice should be tendered to Ministers. As for the proposed pension guarantee and educational trust, he considered that both would require legislation, and he saw no good ground for departing from the views the Treasury had previously expressed on these proposals. His main concern, however, was with the proposal for a British Overseas Service. He was anxious that the British Government should not be induced to enter into long-term and indeed indefinite commitments in order to solve a short-term problem. If the proposed Service were set up, he did not see how it would be possible to resist demands from the existing staffs for equal protection to that extended to new entrants without still further increasing the discontent of serving officers. Any variation of terms of employment for new recruits should be such as could be applied to those already in the Colonial Service. The right approach was to consider what variations within the existing framework could be introduced to allay present discontent and to apply these variations, perhaps with some modifications, to new entrants. There might be a case for setting up a high-level enquiry, possibly to be held in public and with the participation of territorial governments, regarding the basic conditions of the Colonial Service, rather than trying to settle these issues departmentally. He was himself firmly opposed to the creation of any new Service for which the British Government would be responsible.

The Colonial Office staff could not dispute the logic of these views, but maintained that it was simply not possible to wait for the results of an enquiry, which would necessarily take a long time, before doing anything about the immediate problems of the Colonial Service. It was agreed that the Colonial Office should try to work out a scheme which would aim to solve these problems without involving any revolutionary commitment on the part of the British Government. The Office set to work at once, and within a few days had produced the first draft of a statement of policy which formed the basis of subsequent discussions.

As I observed above, while these exchanges were going on between the Colonial Office and the Treasury, the Secretary of State was in Nigeria. The position of the British civil servants necessarily loomed large in the deliberations of the constitutional conference. At a conference held in London in the summer of 1953 it had been agreed that self-government should be given to any of the three Regions of Nigeria which might ask for it from 1956 onwards, subject to the reservation of certain subjects to the Federal government. This arrangement was confirmed at the Lagos conference of January 1954, and there were strong indications which could not be ignored that, unless something effective was done to meet the grievances of the expatriate staffs, there would be a wholesale exodus as soon as regional self-government came into being and the right to retire with compensation became operative. This would be sheer disaster, since the regional governments could not hope to carry on successfully if any substantial proportion of their experienced civil servants were to disappear at the moment when self-government had been attained.

Faced with this gloomy prospect, the Nigerian political leaders decided to do what they could to reassure the European staffs. In a weighty formal statement, after referring to the agreement registered by the conference that officers who wished to retire with compensation should be enabled to do so, they said: 'Nevertheless it is our hope that these officers will stay with us, and we wish to assure them that they need have no anxiety about their future if they do so . . . We hope that as many overseas officers as possible now in the Service will continue to give devoted and valuable service to Nigeria in the new circumstances . . . We intend that all pensions liabilities (including widows' and orphans' benefits) shall be honoured. We assure them that future terms and conditions of service will be fair and reasonable and no less favourable than those obtaining today . . . We fully support the principle that all Public Service questions . . . should be kept completely free and independent of political control. We hope that the traditional principle of promotion according to qualifications, experience, merit, without regard to race will be maintained. We hope these assurances will help to allay the feeling of uncertainty at present existing among overseas officers, and will be accepted by them as an expression of our genuine goodwill. The Nigerian Civil Service has been a partnership in which African and overseas officers work together for a common cause—the good of Nigeria. It is our earnest wish that this same spirit of partnership should continue to animate the new Public Services which are to be established.'

In making this generous and statesmanlike pronouncement the Nigerian politicians had gone as far as it was possible for them to go.

The British civil servants were not unappreciative but it remained a fact that the politicians could not bind future governments of Nigeria and the civil servants maintained their contention that such assurances were not really reliable unless they were specifically underwritten by Her Majesty's Government.

Meanwhile at home other pressures were being brought to bear on the government. Most branches of the Colonial Service had to fight their own battles but the British Medical Association kept a very watchful eye on the interests of its members who belonged to the Colonial Medical Service. During the latter half of 1953 they were asking the Colonial Office for assurances regarding security of tenure, compensation, guarantees of pension, and so forth. This led to a meeting in December at which I was able to explain the position in terms which they accepted as satisfactory, and some useful correspondence followed in the *British Medical Journal*.

In February 1954 Mr Bernard Braine, to whose constructive interest in these problems I have already referred, initiated a series of articles in the fortnightly periodical *New Commonwealth*. In the introductory article he stated the case for a new Commonwealth Service, and this was followed by the record, in subsequent articles, of personal discussions between him and a number of serving or retired officials and Members of Parliament. The first interview was in fact with myself, and I felt it possible to sound a note of cautious confidence in the future of the Colonial Service in some form or another. The continuing overall demand for new recruits seemed to indicate that many territories would need British staffs, particularly specialists, for a long time to come and that losses of opportunities in the more advanced territories would be largely offset by the expansion of public services in those which had further to go on the road to self-government. Others gave their own opinions on the questions put to them by Mr Braine, and in summing up the series in May he concluded that the idea of a joint Commonwealth Service was unrealistic but that there was a very strong case for a single unified Overseas Service based on the United Kingdom, with pay and pensions underwritten by Her Majesty's Government. He called for urgent action along this line. But by the time his article appeared action was already in hand, though not exactly of the kind which he—and some of the Colonial Office staff—would have wished to see.

The feelings of the Colonial Service Division of the Office after the meeting with Sir Edward Bridges in January may fairly be described by the familiar quotation 'bloody but unbowed'. Provided that certain limits were not overstepped, there were a good many useful and necessary things which could now be done without controversy. The first need was to define beyond a doubt the classes of officers towards whom Her Majesty's Government recognized that it had a special responsibility. Membership of one of the unified branches of the Colonial Service was not now an acceptable criterion. Many of the members of these branches were people who had been recruited and were domiciled in the territories in which they were serving, and had acquired membership through local promotion to a scheduled post. This was effectively only a matter of status, since most of them looked for a career in their own countries and were not interested in belonging to an interchangeable Service. Moreover, there were a good many officers scattered about the colonies who had been recruited by the Colonial Office or the Crown Agents for the Colonies but for one reason or another had never been formally appointed to membership of any unified branch; yet they had as much claim as anybody else to such protection as the Secretary of State could give.

A fresh start had, therefore, to be made by drawing up a new and definitive list. This was based on two categories. The first consisted of officers who had been appointed by the Secretary of State to membership of one of the unified branches, who had not ceased to be members of that branch, and who should within six months of the inauguration of the new scheme signify their desire to be included. The second category consisted of other serving officers who were on probation or had been confirmed in pensionable offices, who had been selected by the Secretary of State, who should within the six months signify their desire to be enrolled, and who were recommended for enrolment by their Governor and accepted by the Secretary of State.

This formula ensured not only that the list would be definite but that no serving officer would be put on it except by his own wish. Thus locally domiciled members of the unified branches were not excluded if they wished to join but it was assumed that most of them would feel that their primary loyalty was to their own country and government and would expect to continue in the local public service through any future constitutional changes.

The next need was to find a new corporate title for the officers to be included in the list and, following a suggestion which had been made during the Nigerian discussions, it was decided to propose, subject to the Queen's approval, 'Her Majesty's Oversea Civil Service'. (At this time the Colonial Office was accustomed to use 'oversea' as an adjective and 'overseas' as an adverb; later it became more usual to write 'overseas' as the adjective and the title of the Service was amended accordingly in 1956.)

These were formalities, though by no means unimportant. The real question was what rights, privileges, or protection members of

HMOCS would enjoy which were not already available to them as members of the Colonial Service. The answer was, frankly, few or none so long as Her Majesty's Government remained responsible for the territories in which they were serving: the necessary safeguards were already there in the Colonial Regulations and the local constitutional instruments. It was when a territory became independent that the practical issue would arise. At that stage officers were entitled to expect that, so long as they should continue to serve, their terms of service would not be altered to their disadvantage; that their pensions and those of their dependants would be safeguarded; that they should still be regarded as members of Her Majesty's service and eligible for transfer or promotion to other territories, and that their employing government would not stand in the way of their accepting such transfer or promotion and would preserve their existing pension rights on transfer; that they would be given adequate notice of any intention to terminate their employment in consequence of constitutional changes, and that in that event the British Government would try to find them other jobs if they so wished; and that if prematurely retired on account of constitutional changes they would receive compensation from the government of the territory concerned.

It was proposed that the statement of policy should set forth these legitimate requirements and embody a solemn declaration by Her Majesty's Government of their intention, if and when any territory should attain self-government, to ensure the observance of these conditions by a formal agreement with the government of the territory. The agreement would also provide for the continuing payment of pensions already awarded to officers and their dependants.

In the matter of pensions the Colonial Office did not feel able to press further, against the firm opposition of the Treasury, the case for a specific guarantee by the British Government. In spite of the importance attached to this point in some Colonial Service quarters the fears which had been expressed could not be considered as very well justified. If a future independent territorial government could go back on the agreement, so, in theory, might some future British Parliament. Whatever was written or not written there must be an element of trust. It was not really thinkable that if the other party to such an agreement should default Her Majesty's Government would leave the pensioners from Her Majesty's Service to suffer the consequences.

The Treasury officials, anxious to be as helpful as possible within the limits of what they regarded as the correct approach, fully agreed to support proposals along these lines. The Colonial Office was grateful for this, but felt that, while the scheme would, it was hoped, help to restore the confidence of serving officers, it could do little or nothing to help in solving the problem of the future staffing of the territories, which was at least as important. Recruitment was still proceeding at an undiminished rate to meet the demands of the colonial governments. Prospective recruits would be looking not so much for assurances about what would happen when their jobs came to an end as for assurances that the Service offered opportunities for a worthwhile career for a reasonable length of time to come.

As I have observed in the Prologue, the Colonial Office technically existed only as the instrument of the Secretary of State for the time being, but as a continuous institution it had in fact a corporate 'mind' of its own, built up on its long tradition, the experience and personal characters of its staff, and the effectual influence of its constant and intimate contact with the Colonial Service. At the time of the events now being chronicled the Colonial Office mind was working somewhat as follows. It was now clear that within a few years most or all of the larger colonial territories would become independent, or at least would reach a constitutional stage at which it would be practically impossible for the Secretary of State to intervene on behalf of any civil servant, or group of civil servants, in the employment of the territorial government. It was also clear that, throughout this stage and in many cases after full independence had been achieved, the territories would need and would wish to employ expatriate staffs in a wide range of administrative and specialist posts calling for experience and skill not as yet possessed by sufficient numbers of local people. Not only would they want to retain their present staffs but they would require to recruit fresh staff to fill vacancies. Up to then these needs had been met by the Colonial Service, and its work had been appreciated by the peoples of the territories and their leaders who, by all indications, were very happy that British officers should continue to serve them, provided that they did not have to employ an officer unless they wanted to and could terminate his employment when they no longer needed him.

With the winding up of the Colonial Empire now coming into sight, the Colonial Office felt a strong sense of responsibility. Great issues would turn on the attitude of the emerging independent nations towards Britain. From the point of view of the territories themselves, no less than from the British point of view, the colonial episode would only have made sense if it resulted in the new countries and the old country continuing as friends and partners when the ruler-subject relationship should come to an end. It could by no means be taken for granted that such a result would spring from a sense of loyalty to the British Crown on the part of the colonial peoples or from gratitude for the rather belated expenditure of money by the British taxpayer on colonial development and welfare. But at least the British could do their part by seeing that, when the time came, the new countries would start off with a democratic system of government backed by an efficient judiciary, civil service, and police force impartial and independent of political control. In establishing such a system and the social and economic services essential to a modern state, British officers could make an invaluable and indeed an indispensable contribution. Whatever the outcome, it should never be possible for anyone to say that Britain had let her colonies down because she was unable or unwilling to supply British officers to meet their staffing needs in their time of crisis. Any cost to the British taxpayer would be insignificant in relation to the issues at stake and to the magnitude of the sums already being spent on aid to the territories.

The Colonial Office was convinced that, if the opportunities were not to be lost, there would have to be a departure from the traditional arrangement whereby there was no establishment to which an officer could belong except that of the government of the territory in which he was serving. The Office therefore urged that the statement of policy to be issued, having dealt with the position of existing members of the Colonial Service as proposed, should at least indicate acceptance in principle of the intention that in future, as circumstances might require, officers should be recruited into HMOCS as direct employees of Her Majesty's Government, for assignment on loan to territorial governments at the direction of the Secretary of State. The Treasury however firmly maintained their objection to any commitment along these lines, but they agreed that the statement could include a reference to the ideas of a Commonwealth Service or a British Overseas Service which had been aired publicly, and say that the present decisions were not intended to exclude such developments should they be found desirable and practicable. It would be pointed out that the question involved many difficulties which would need much consideration, so that an immediate conclusion was not possible.

It was now March 1954 and the need for an early statement of some kind became daily more pressing. The Colonial Office felt that it was impossible to delay matters for further argument about the future and that the right course was to proceed urgently with the very important measures on which agreement had been reached. The Secretary of State (Mr Lyttelton) accepted this view, and the statement which had been drafted was referred confidentially to a number of senior Governors. In general they welcomed it warmly, so far as it went. Some doubted whether it would go far enough to satisfy the misgivings of the Service, and there was a strong feeling that the establishment of a central Service operated by Her Majesty's Government would be simpler and more acceptable to the Service and the territorial governments.

On 2 April a debate took place in the House of Commons on a motion by Mr C. J. M. (afterwards Lord) Alport calling for a reorganization of the respective spheres and responsibilities of the Colonial Office and the Commonwealth Relations office. In the course of the debate several references were made to the Colonial Service. Mr Alport suggested that the present Service should be placed on a regional basis, so as to make the best use of officers' local experience, and that a new Service, not part of the existing Service, should be created to provide expert technical advice and assistance, both to the colonies and to developing countries which had achieved or might achieve independence.

In seconding the motion Mr Bernard Braine referred to the uncertainty and doubt in the minds of Colonial Service officers and to the extent to which recruitment was failing to meet the demand for expatriate staff. In 1951 the Secretary of State had made 1396 appointments, but at the end of the year there were 988 unfilled vacancies. The corresponding figures for 1952 were 1378 and 1055; and for 1953, 1227 and 1048. The present set-up, he said, was quite inadequate. What was needed was a new and unified Service. The United Kingdom should contribute to its cost, the balance being provided by the employing governments in proportion to their financial resources and not to the number of expatriate officers whom they employed. Expense should not stand in the way. 'We are moving', he said, 'into a new, delicate and difficult phase in Commonwealth relations, and we cannot afford not to have the best men training the colonial cadres. The colonial servant is far more than an envoy for this country. His job is to forge the links of mutual trust and understanding that alone can ensure that the Commonwealth holds together. It is the quality of the colonial servant's work, the confidence he inspires, the example he sets, that will determine whether some of the new States will decide to stay within the family circle or not.' It was imperative to do something about the Colonial Service before it was too late.

Mr T. Reid, himself a former member of the Colonial Service, was not altogether in agreement about the suggested remedy. He thought it inevitable that the public services of the territories in the future would be staffed by their own nationals. Mr I. Winterbottom, who had recently visited West Africa, had been much impressed by the poor morale of the officers there, owing to uncertainty about their position. He felt that, while the assurances given by Dr Nkrumah and the Nigerian leaders were satisfactory as far as they went, more was needed. He urged the creation of a new Overseas Civil Service and acceptance by

Her Majesty's Government of liability for expatriation pay. Sir Patrick Spens said that every effort should be made to transform the Colonial Service into a Commonwealth Service. Mr T. L. Iremonger, another former member of the Colonial Service, referred to the peculiarly difficult position of the British officers in relation to the peoples of the countries in which they were serving, inasmuch as they had to be at the same time rulers and servants. He paid tribute to the good work done by the officers in spite of 'being run by an office and organised in a series of services which are illogical and chaotic and rapidly becoming demoralised'.

Replying to the debate the Minister of State for the Colonies, Mr Henry Hopkinson (afterwards Lord Colyton), accepted the need for an urgent review of Colonial Service conditions. Her Majesty's Government recognized that they had a special responsibility towards the Service: it was a complicated problem and was under active examination. 'We cannot', he concluded, 'overestimate the debt which this country and the colonial territories owe to the devoted and efficient work of the men and women who are serving in the colonies. We believe there is still a great work for them to do. We want them to know that this House and government are aware of their needs and we are determined to give them every practical assistance for carrying on their great task.'

Finally Mr J. Tilney expressed the hope that Her Majesty's Government would consider helping the Colonial Service to be sure of at any rate a portion of their pensions and pay. The Colonial Development and Welfare fund might, he suggested, be used to provide for expatriation pay.

The debate was helpful in bringing the needs and difficulties of the Colonial Service into the light and encouraging the growth of public opinion in favour of recognizing that the British Government had a special responsibility for looking after the interests of its officers. The particular suggestions made in the debate were duly noted but they could not have much practical effect on the action which was now under way. There was a good deal that had to be done, and no time to be lost.

The statement of policy, having been got into its final form in the light of the preliminary soundings, agreed with the Treasury, and approved by the Secretary of State, had next, as a matter of courtesy and wisdom, to be sent out in advance to the Governors of the colonies, so that they should know what was planned and have the opportunity of making any comments before publication. This was put in hand, with a deadline in May for any observations. It was fully realized that much depended on the timing and manner of the presentation of the new policy to the Service. It would not be difficult for a cynical critic to claim that, apart from the change of title, there was not much in the constitution of HMOCS which was not already available for the Colonial Service. It was therefore of prime importance to focus attention on the positive features of the statement, which in fact were quite novel and substantial. First there was the explicit recognition on the part of the British Government of its special obligation to the officers who had been recruited by the Secretary of State. This had never been stated in so many words before, and while the steps immediately proposed for implementing this obligation were not very spectacular acceptance of the principle committed the British Government to take whatever further action might prove to be necessary in the light of future developments. Secondly there was the extension of this acknowledged obligation to officers who were not members of any of the unified branches if they owed their appointments to selection by the Secretary of State. Then there was the definite undertaking that when a territory should attain self-government the British Government would secure a formal agreement guaranteeing the conditions of service and the pensions of all officers enrolled in HMOCS. Most important of all, the new scheme provided for the first time a ready-made framework which could conveniently be adapted to provide for a centrally organized and paid Service if events should work out that way. The Colonial Office felt that much indeed had been gained and that, as Mr D. S. Senanayake said to the Ceylon State Council on a historic occasion, 'a man should not refuse bread merely because it is not cake'.

In the hope that the Colonial Service and the public would see the new departure in this light, and in order to give HMOCS the best possible start, Mr Lyttelton wished to seize the opportunity to launch the new Service in his presidential speech at the annual Colonial Service dinner of the Corona Club on 18 June. This meant that he should make a brief statement in the House of Commons earlier in the day, drawing attention to the White Paper (Colonial No. 306) published simultaneously, entitled *Reorganisation of the Colonial Service*. Meanwhile the document had to be got into its final form, printing arranged, the concurrence of other Cabinet Ministers obtained, the Queen's approval sought for the new title, colonial governments alerted, and the necessary briefing for press and publicity prepared. It was a bit of a scramble at the end but all was done in time.

The Corona Club was (and is) an institution founded by Joseph Chamberlain in 1900 with the object of providing an annual dinner (quaintly described in the original constitution as a 'smoking conversazione') in London at which past and present members of the Colonial Service and the Colonial Office could meet and talk and exchange experiences and ideas with each other and with the Secretary of State for the time being, who always presided and made the one speech permitted by the custom of the Club. The text of the speech was afterwards circulated to all members of the Club. Some three hundred retired and serving officers actually attended the dinners, the press was represented, and anything which the Secretary of State might say, over and above the customary platitudes, attracted a good deal of attention and publicity in quarters interested in colonial affairs. Lord Passfield chose the occasion of the Corona Club dinner in 1930 to announce the unification of the Colonial Service. It was fully appropriate that Mr Lyttelton should take a similar opportunity to announce the transformation of the Colonial Service into Her Majesty's Oversea Civil Service in 1954.

'This very day', he said, 'a Colonial Office paper was available to Members of the House of Commons in the Vote Office, and tomorrow morning no doubt it will excite some comment in the Press ... The title of that paper is "Reorganisation of the Colonial Service". The paper, which has to be brief, is the result of many months' work. The difficulties which have called for a re-examination of the structure of the Colonial Service arise out of constitutional developments which either have taken place or are expected to take place in certain territories, and of course, it is quite clear that as progress towards self-government is made, the powers of control conferred upon the Secretary of State must in practice be modified.

'A territory cannot be given self-government and the Colonial Secretary retain the strings in his own hands.

'Therefore two lines of action appear to us to be essential. First where a new constitution is under discussion, as for example, in Nigeria, necessary safeguards for the public service should be embodied in the constitutional instruments. This has been done, and I think the more those arrangements are studied by Colonial Civil Servants the more their confidence in their future in these territories will be underwritten and confirmed. Their skill and advice and experience are, I readily believe, recognised by everyone to be necessary if the evolution to self-government is to take place smoothly and if that self-government when it is reached is to fulfil the principles of good government which we have at heart.

'There is a second feature in this problem. What is to happen in these territories which in the fairly near future achieve independence of any control by Her Majesty's Government in the United Kingdom? I believe that in general they will want to go on having the help of their friends who have served them so well, and that the officers of the Colonial Service too will for the most part be anxious to carry on with the work they know and love. But of course there will be some officers who cannot stay on yet do not want to retire, and Her Majesty's Government, as far as lies in their power, must do their best to find other posts for them. It is, of course, clear that we cannot guarantee other work for them, but we must do our best.

'Let me interpolate here that although I regard it as certain and indeed desirable that the proportion or percentage of oversea Civil Servants finding work in the whole of the Colonial territories will decline in relation to those locally recruited, that is not at all the same thing as imagining that the absolute numbers of oversea Civil Servants will decline. They may in particular territories but it is, of course, well known to you that we have been recruiting five times as many men and women every year as we did before the war. The rate may not keep up quite to that figure but I don't think it is likely to go down very much for a long time yet. After all what other conclusion can you reach if you study for a moment some of the figures of the economic development of some of these territories? It bears out my argument when we remember, for instance, that in 1920 the traffic on the Kenya–Uganda Railway was less than a quarter of a million tons, and in 1952 it carried just over $4\frac{1}{2}$ million tons: that is multiplying the freight carried by more than 18 times; and again, Nigeria's total import and export trade in 1920 was no more than £38m. In 1953, it was £233m.

'But to revert to today's statement of policy, we are going to have a new name—Her Majesty's Oversea Civil Service, and this will replace the unified branches of the Colonial Civil Service. The new Service will include members of those branches and other officers who are selected by the Secretary of State.

'This does not, of course, in any way imply that we shall overlook the rights and interests of the many pensionable overseas officers who do not fall within this definition. The terms and conditions of their employment vary too much to make it possible to bring them all within a single framework.

'Now, is this new name to be more than a name? I assure you that it is. The creation of the new Service carries highly important practical implications. The new Service is a definable body, differing from the much more loosely defined body such as is the Colonial Service today. It carries on into the new era the status and traditions of the Colonial Service as one of the great Services of the Crown.

'Secondly, once an officer has been enrolled as a member of Her Majesty's Oversea Civil Service, he will be kept on the books and wherever he may be he can be considered for any suitable employment which Her Majesty's Government may be able to offer and Her

Majesty's Government will continue to have an interest in his career and in his welfare.

'The main object, then, of this new deal is to make clear the position of present members of the unified Colonial Service and to create a firm foundation upon which they can build their future careers. I hope, too, that it will stimulate recruitment, and that it will give the finest possible encouragement to young men and women to come forward and carry on the great tradition which so many of you here have bequeathed or are now bequeathing to posterity.

'I might also mention that other Governments do occasionally ask us to lend officers to them for particular tasks, and of course members of Her Majesty's Oversea Civil Service would be among the first to be considered for work like this.

'You will have seen, My Lords and Gentlemen, various ideas canvassed in the Press and elsewhere about the possibility of starting some entirely new Commonwealth or Oversea Service. Our statement shows that we do not rule out such a possibility, but, as you well know, there are many constitutional and practical difficulties about such a proposal, and all I can say now is that we have not come to a point at which we could say for certain that it would be wise to embark upon such an adventure today. But the new step we have taken at least clears up the present position of the Colonial Service, and from this vantage point we can study the wider implications which the wider proposals may open up to us.

'The new Service has inherited—and I repeat it with a sincerity which I claim is founded upon knowledge and experience of their work—a glorious tradition which I know that it will carry forward and once again embellish in new ways.'

It was one of Mr Lyttelton's last important acts as Secretary of State. In July 1954 he retired from the Government and was succeeded by Mr Alan Lennox-Boyd.

7

DAMP SQUIB

The second half of 1954 was occupied with the practical work involved in translating into action the policy laid down in Colonial No. 306. Explanatory memoranda had to be circulated to the colonial governments, arrangements organized for collecting the names of the officers to be enrolled in the new Service, decisions given on a host of queries about the interpretation and application of the rules in particular cases. In general the reception of the scheme by the Service was favourable: even the Colonial Civil Servants' Association could scarce forbear to cheer. Predictably, however, the reaction in West Africa, and especially in Nigeria, was one of disappointment rather than of appreciation. So far as the officers there were concerned, the new policy, in their own words, proved a 'damp squib'. It was all very well for the British Government to promise to obtain agreements from the governments of territories which should become independent, but this did not, in the officers' opinion, touch the real problem. In Nigeria there was not, as yet, any plan for conferring independence on the country as a whole, but it was reasonably certain that regional self-government would come into operation in or soon after 1956. The European civil servants felt that this would put them in a seriously anomalous position. It was not clear that the scheme for making agreements with independent governments could be applied to the regions, and the officers did not put much faith in paper agreements anyhow. As civil servants they would have to carry out the policies of the regional Ministers, whether or not they thought those policies wise or practical, and it was only too likely that, if things then went wrong, they would be made scapegoats.

This was also the period during which Mr Lennox-Boyd was settling in to his new job. He was no stranger to the Colonial Office. As Minister of State in 1951–52 he had devoted himself enthusiastically to his work and, when he left to become Minister of Transport, he made no secret of his hope that some day he would return to the Office. The colonies and the Colonial Service knew that in him they had a good and effective friend. He was fully convinced that in the critical period through which the colonies were passing the maintenance of an efficient and contented Colonial Service was a matter of the highest priority. He well understood and was deeply concerned about the problems of the Service.

At the beginning of 1955 Mr Lennox-Boyd visited West Africa. His consultations with Governors and senior officials left him in no doubt that, so far at any rate as that area was concerned, the palliatives embodied in the 1954 statement of policy were wholly insufficient to meet the case. It was widely held that the change to HMOCS was one of name only; officers felt that nothing had been added to their security. In the Gold Coast the position was described as well-nigh desperate; in spite of the safeguards included in the constitution, experienced officers were leaving and there were no qualified Africans available to replace them. In Nigeria the situation was worse. It was strongly urged upon the Secretary of State that, unless a Service based on the United Kingdom were set up, Her Majesty's Government might well find itself unable to continue to fulfil its obligations to the West African territories.

The effects of the delays in reaching agreement on the future of the Colonial Service had been most marked in West Africa. The doubt and uncertainty had made it particularly difficult to fill posts in the administrative service. As Table II shows between 1951 and 1955 there had been a very dramatic increase in the percentage of administrative posts unfilled in West Africa—from 34 to 83 per cent—and this increase seemed to represent a general trend already being felt in Eastern and Central Africa. There were even marginal increases in the proportion of unfilled posts to be found in other branches of the Colonial Service.

TABLE II. Colonial Service Posts Unfilled, 1951, 1953, and 1955

	1951 %	1953 %	1955 %
A. *Administrative Posts*			
West Africa	34	51	83
East and Central Africa	37	42	62
Southeast Asia	23	27	27
Rest of the Empire	26	29	46
B. *All Other Posts*			
West Africa	47	53	53
East and Central Africa	37	41	45
Southeast Asia	48	39	43
Rest of the Empire	41	63	43

Source: Annual Progress Reports, Colonial Service Division (see Appendix III).

The Secretary of State took the representations from West Africa very seriously, and instructed the Office staff to do its utmost to find a solution. One of the difficulties that had to be faced was the proverbial one that hard cases make bad laws. In general the HMOCS scheme was so far working well. It was only in West Africa, and more particularly in Nigeria—and indeed most particularly in the Eastern Region of that territory—that significant problems had arisen. Was it right to upset a whole going concern, after only a few months of trial, in order to deal with a local and temporary situation, with no certainty of success even there? The answer to this seemed to be that the same kind of trouble as had developed in Nigeria was quite likely to crop up in other territories as the move towards independence went forward; the aim, therefore, should be to devise some remedy for Nigeria which could be applied elsewhere as and when required.

Various ideas were examined, some coming from within the Colonial Office, some contributed from other sources. One suggestion was that the British Government should offer a block grant in aid of administration, guaranteed for five years and based on the number of expatriate officers actually employed in the territory concerned. This would avoid the risk of creating divided loyalties, since the officers would remain the servants of the territorial government. It would provide an inducement to the local governments to keep up their staffs of expatriate officers and to give them reasonable terms of service, and so would encourage the officers to feel contented and secure. It was, however, admitted that such a scheme would be difficult to get through and would not satisfy the growing demand for a home-based Service.

Another idea was that during the transitional period between internal self-government and full independence officers should be given a joint guarantee by the British and territorial governments, with an additional provision that an officer who lost his job would receive full pay from the British Government for up to a year while awaiting another posting. A further suggestion was that the British Government should promise a gratuity or bonus to officers who were willing to stay on rather than take the opportunity to retire early with compensation.

These ideas, and any others that anyone could produce, were exhaustively discussed within the Colonial Office and in correspondence and conversation between the Office and the authorities in Nigeria during the summer of 1955. It became abundantly clear that no compromise along such lines would be acceptable in Nigeria. Local political resistance would be fatal to any scheme for a subsidy designed to facilitate the employment of expatriate staff. Officers would not have confidence in agreements entered into by the existing ministerial governments. If it were argued that the Nigerian politicians should be left to learn the hard way, the plain fact was that this could not be afforded. Nothing less was at stake than the continued existence of effective public services in Nigeria and the future of Nigeria as an organized state. If the present staffs left they could not be replaced and the administration of the country would irretrievably break down. Considerable numbers of officers were already intending to quit when regional self-government came into force in 1956. Any new scheme which was mere window-dressing would do more harm than good; the only solution was to set up a service which would be Her Majesty's in fact as well as in name. Although the main difficulties at the moment occurred in the Eastern Region, where Ministers were openly (if not very realistically) proclaiming their intention to introduce a hundred per cent Africanization on attaining self-government, there were strong objections to any attempt to deal with the problem in this Region in isolation from the rest of the Nigerian services.

In short, the question confronting the British Government was neatly summed up by one of the Governors when he exclaimed, in a moment of exasperation, 'Do they want to keep the bloody place or not?' The Colonial Office knew what it wanted, and strove to find a practicable way. The outline of a plan began to take shape. While there should be no general disturbance of the organization of HMOCS, provision might be made for a 'Special Division' of that Service, the members of which would be in the direct employment of Her Majesty's Government in the United Kingdom. The difference between this plan and earlier proposals for a British Overseas Service was that the Special Division would be within the framework of HMOCS, and membership would be offered only to officers in territories approaching self-government.

This plan seemed to promise a possible solution if it could be worked out. The terms of employment in the Special Division would clearly have to be attractive enough to induce officers to accept offers of transfer to it, and these would have to be negotiated; but first it would be necessary to settle the basic issue of principle, that is how far, if at all, Her Majesty's Government should accept any specific commitment.

The idea of the Special Division came to birth as a result of discussions between the Colonial Office and a visiting deputation of senior Nigerian officials in June 1955. Various possibilities were examined, but the Nigerian representatives stuck to their considered view that nothing short of a home-based Service would at that stage prove successful in averting a fatal exodus of European staff. The Colonial Office was in the position of recognizing at one and the same time the validity of the Nigerian arguments and the logical force of the Treasury's objections. Further representations were made to the Treasury, and at a meeting on 11 July Sir Edward Bridges, while maintaining his firm opposition to setting up any new United Kingdom Service, agreed to the idea of a Special List for which Her Majesty's Government should accept a special responsibility. That responsibility, he considered, might take the form of the United Kingdom taking over the payment of pensions and compensation on an agency basis, and agreeing to pay salary for up to a year to a displaced officer who could not immediately be found other employment.

These were important and constructive concessions but, when the plan was put in this form to the Governor-General of Nigeria, Sir James Robertson, he flatly rejected it as quite inadequate to meet the situation. No further progress was possible until October, when the Secretary of State convened a meeting of the Governor-General and the Regional Governors at the Colonial Office to review the arrangements for regional self-government in 1956 and the future progress towards independence for the whole territory. The question of the public services was necessarily in the forefront of the discussions. During the period of preparation for the conference numerous consultations took place between Colonial Office and Treasury officials in order to see how far it was possible to go with an agreed policy. The Treasury sought to be helpful but their approach was inevitably that summed up by Sir Edward Bridges in one of our conversations. 'My concern', he said, 'is where we are going to stop.'

However, as a result of these exchanges I was able to place before the conference when it assembled a 'new formula for HMOCS' which had been discussed with Sir Edward and had received, if not his approval, his consent to its being offered for consideration. The main lines of this formula were as follows. HMOCS would be defined as a Service of the Crown. Members would be appointed to the Service by Her Majesty's Government and assigned by Her Majesty's Government for duty under overseas governments. Membership would be conferred by the Secretary of State on such persons as he might, with their consent, select. It would carry no emolument or privilege except as stated in the rest of the document.

The procedure for assignment would be that the Secretary of State would make an offer to a member of a post on the terms provided by the overseas government. On the member's acceptance, the overseas government would be requested to take the officer into its employment on the agreed terms and on the understanding that the terms would not be altered to the officer's disadvantage and that the salaries and other conditions provided from time to time would be maintained at a level not less favourable than that which might be prescribed by

Her Majesty's Government as reasonable in current circumstances. While the terms were primarily a matter for the overseas government, if Her Majesty's Government should decide (after due consultation) that the terms applied to any officer or class of officers were not reasonable, it would take steps to ensure reasonable terms or would at its discretion offer the officer concerned alternative employment. Failing this, it would require the overseas government to allow the officer to retire with compensation on a scale approved by Her Majesty's Government. Her Majesty's Government would accept responsibility for all pensions to members and their dependants, recovering the cost from the overseas governments. Members having to leave their jobs owing to abolition of office, constitutional changes, or failure to provide reasonable terms would be allowed to remain on full pensionable pay for up to a year from the expiry of earned leave while awaiting another assignment. The pay for any such period would be refunded to the oversea government by Her Majesty's Government.

Sir Edward Bridges had made it clear that the Treasury would object to any proposals involving the possibility of Her Majesty's Government providing a subsidy to supplement emoluments considered to be unreasonably low. Pressure should be put on the employing governments to give reasonable conditions: if this should fail, then, in the Treasury view, officers could only be advised to leave.

The Nigerian Governors were not much impressed by this formula. They pointed out that the paramount need was to induce officers to stay, and they did not think that this scheme offered sufficient inducement. Officers wanted an assurance not only of reasonable conditions but of continuing employment up to normal retiring age. Otherwise they would prefer to get out with compensation before it was too late for them to find fresh ways of earning a living.

Mr Lennox-Boyd felt obliged to accept the Governors' view of the situation. He agreed that positive action by Her Majesty's Government was essential and felt that any cost involved was unlikely to be excessive and should in any case be weighed against the clear and substantial United Kingdom interest in maintaining a stable administration and the British connection in Nigeria. To disregard these considerations would be to risk a major defeat for British colonial policy. He instructed his officials to get together with the Governor-General and the Governors and work out an agreed scheme which he could place before his colleagues.

The general outline of such a scheme was very quickly agreed upon. At a stated date officers in the service of a government to which the scheme would be applied (for example a regional government in Nigeria) would have the option of continuing in their existing service, retaining such rights as they might have to retirement with compensation, or of transferring to the service of Her Majesty's Government. Scales of pay and allowances would previously have been drawn up, and each officer would know at what point he would be assimilated to these scales if he should opt for transfer. All emoluments would be paid directly to the officer by the British Government; they would be recovered from the government employing the officer. Officers not employed overseas would receive salary but not overseas allowance. Tenure of appointment would cease at the age of fifty (this was substituted in discussion for forty-five) unless previously terminated on account of ill-health, resignation, misconduct, refusal to accept an assignment, or acceptance of transfer to another public service. There would be a Provident Fund to which Her Majesty's Government would contribute a percentage of the officer's pay to accumulate at compound interest, the proceeds to be paid to the officer on his retirement or to his dependants in the event of his death. (In discussion it was agreed that an alternative of pension should be made available.)

This outline having been concurred in by the Governors, the next thing was to put up a detailed plan to the Secretary of State. This was worked out in two parts. The first part was to apply to HMOCS as a whole. The main points were:

Her Majesty's Government would be empowered to take over, by agreement with an overseas government, the payment of all pensions due from that government to officers or their dependants, and to recover the payments from that government;

An officer out of a job through no fault of his own before reaching retirement age would receive full pay from Her Majesty's Government at his last colonial rate up to a year from the expiry of his earned leave;

There would be an educational trust fund available to all members of HMOCS on the basis of individual need. £1m would be provided to cover the first ten years, subject to review after five years in the light of experience.

The second part of the scheme applied to territories approaching self-government. In these cases Her Majesty's Government would be empowered to enter into an agreement with the government concerned for the offer to all officers of HMOCS currently employed in the territory of transfer to a 'Special Division' on terms which were, broadly speaking, those which had been agreed with the Nigerian Governors (that is to say, including an option to transfer to the service of Her Majesty's Government) but with the additional provision that officers should be given, once for all at the time of transfer, an option of pensionability under the United Kingdom Superannuation Acts as an alternative to the proposed Provident fund.

This plan was submitted to the Secretary of State with full support from Sir Thomas Lloyd. Mr Lennox-Boyd thoroughly approved and decided to send it to the Chancellor of the Exchequer, Mr R. A. (afterwards Lord) Butler, with a warm covering letter. The definitive version of the Colonial Office proposals was completed by the end of October, and on 1 November the Secretary of State despatched his letter to the Chancellor.

While all this was going on, the Colonial Office officials naturally kept in touch with their colleagues in the Treasury, and often found themselves in a somewhat unenviable position, with the Treasury feeling that the Colonial Office was too easily persuaded by the militant Nigerian Governors, and the latter feeling that the Colonial Office took too much notice of the Treasury objections. The Treasury men indeed were by no means unhelpful or unsympathetic. They remained, however, firmly opposed to the idea of transfer to the service of Her Majesty's Government—which was, of course, the key point in the representations of the Nigerian officers.

Any hopes which Mr Lennox-Boyd may have entertained of breaching the Treasury walls by a personal approach were heavily damped by the Chancellor's reply, sent on 10 November. Mr Butler, while agreeing that the problem was an important and difficult one, said that he was greatly disturbed by the proposals for its solution. He foresaw that a commitment to give officers employment or pay up to age 50 might result in the British government being saddled with an obligation to pay a large number of persons for many years for doing nothing. There seemed to be very little chance of absorbing into other government employment all the officers who were likely to be affected as the process of granting independence to colonies went forward; he did not feel that the proposal for paying officers for up to a year in case of unemployment should apply to HMOCS as a whole; and he thought that the educational trust fund if created might encourage overseas governments to disown their normal obligations to expatriate staff. Mr Butler was by no means convinced that the scheme would be acceptable to overseas governments: might the British not be accused of seeking to maintain a specially paid staff for imperialistic purposes? Nor was he convinced that the scheme would be successful in inducing officers to stay on in Eastern Nigeria. He could not accept that, if it failed in this object, the officers should all come home and be paid by Her Majesty's Government until they should reach the age of 50. He considered, therefore, that the right course was to concentrate on Nigeria and in particular the Eastern Region. The Treasury had already gone a long way to meet the Colonial Office, and the measures to which they had agreed ought to be given a trial now in Nigeria. Should they prove inadequate, further steps should be considered, including the use of reserved powers. It was not much more than a year since HMOCS had been established: it should have a fair trial and not have its shape permanently distorted in order to deal with a temporary crisis in one territory. He hoped that the Secretary of State would not press his proposals.

Mr Lennox-Boyd's reaction, as expressed in his reply to the Chancellor, was one of acute disappointment. He felt that his whole point had been missed, namely that it was indeed necessary to change the shape of HMOCS, not only to meet a temporary crisis in Nigeria, but to make it possible for a British service to continue there and in other places where advanced constitutions had been or would soon be introduced. The time for such action was now, while there was still a chance. The Treasury plan had already been rejected as inadequate by the Nigerian Governor-General and Governors: to put it forward as the best that Her Majesty's Government could do might well wreck the Service in Nigeria. It was for the Secretary of State to be the best judge of the use of reserved powers, and he could not possibly at that juncture employ them for imposing conditions of service for British officials. He must, therefore, press his proposals as a matter of the highest policy comparable in importance to the introduction of Colonial Development and Welfare in 1940. As such, he wished to refer the matter to the Colonial Policy Committee of the Cabinet.

The Chancellor, while regretting that he and the Secretary of State were still so far apart, did not move very far towards an agreement. He pointed out, with justice, that the Treasury had made very substantial concessions of principle. For years they had resisted the central payment of pensions and compensation and the acceptance of any financial liability by Her Majesty's Government for the Colonial Service. All that had now been conceded. He still felt that the situation should be dealt with by special measures for Nigeria, coupled with a scheme broadly agreed with the Treasury. He hoped that further efforts would be made to reach agreement before reference to the Colonial Policy Committee, on which the Treasury was not represented, and which, therefore, was not the obvious forum for discussing a matter in which questions of establishment and finance bulked so largely.

Mr Lennox-Boyd wrote back assuring his colleague that he really did appreciate the Treasury concessions but maintaining that they did not go far enough. Administration and finance were really secondary issues: the main issue was one of major policy. The Governor-General and Governors had made it clear that no formula of 'assignment' not incorporating the principle of transfer to the direct employment of Her Majesty's Government would be acceptable. Special measures for Eastern Nigeria (or for Eastern and Western Nigeria) alone would not be effective unless they included that principle. Nor would such measures be acceptable to the regional governments if they took the form of singling out those Regions for special treatment. If the principle were conceded—which he regarded as absolutely essential—there was everything to be said for doing it as part of a constructive general policy which could be applied without further legislation to the rest of Nigeria and in due course to other places as might prove to be necessary. His proposals were designed not only to meet the need of serving officers in Nigeria but to provide an organization into which recruits could be attracted. He had an open mind on the details. His only stipulation was that the terms must be generous enough to induce officers to stay on, and that whatever was done should be done quickly, as there was very little time to lose.

At the same time Mr Lennox-Boyd wrote to the Prime Minister (Mr Anthony Eden, afterwards Lord Avon), to put him in the picture as Chairman of the Colonial Policy Committee.

While these exchanges were taking place during November, the Governor-General of Nigeria, Sir James Robertson, was becoming increasingly worried by the delay. He wrote to the Colonial Office that men were trickling away and, so far as the public and the Service were aware, nothing seemed to be being done. He himself knew of the battle which the Colonial Office was fighting but it was becoming more and more urgent that some results should be visible.

After the receipt of Mr Lennox-Boyd's letter at the Treasury, there were further discussions at the official level in order to clarify certain points. The Treasury made it clear that they still did not like the general scheme. Eventually, on 21 December, Mr Butler sent his reply. He felt it to be a major difficulty that the proposed acceptance by Her Majesty's Government of an obligation to find officers work or pay up to the age of 50 would mean in effect the transfer of liability to compensate officers for loss of career to the British government from the overseas government on which the liability properly rested.

This must have been one of the last letters signed by Mr Butler as Chancellor of the Exchequer, for at this precise juncture one of those periodical twists of the kaleidoscope of power altered the picture. Mr Butler left the Treasury to become Leader of the House of Commons, and Mr Harold Macmillan crossed the street from the Foreign Office to the Chancellor's seat. Unlike his predecessor, Mr Macmillan was not without direct experience of the Colonial Office and its problems. His brief but lively spell as Parliamentary Under-Secretary of State in 1942 had left its mark on him and on the Office. It was with renewed confidence that Mr Lennox-Boyd wrote to him asking for an early discussion as soon as he had settled down to his new duties.

The Colonial Office felt, rightly or wrongly, that the real difficulty underlying the Treasury's attitude was the idea of setting up yet another civil service for which her Majesty's Government would be responsible but over which it would not have effective control, since establishments, postings, and conditions of employment would necessarily depend on decisions by overseas governments. As for the ostensible difficulty, namely the uncertainty of the prospective financial liability, the Colonial Office thought that it could fairly be pointed out that the liability, while admittedly uncertain, was not infinite. A hundred unemployed officers paid at an average rate of £1000 a year would cost the taxpayer £100,000. The Colonial Office felt that, even if this cost were doubled or trebled it would not be a very heavy price to pay for saving Nigeria (and not Nigeria alone) for the Commonwealth. Although Nigeria had tended to monopolize attention, it was not the only country concerned. Something might yet be saved in the Gold Coast. A formal conference had been arranged to take place in January 1956 to decide the future of the Federation of Malaya, with a view to the grant of independence at an early date. The same kind of questions as had arisen in Nigeria would undoubtedly come up.

It was not, however, the extent of the financial commitment which troubled the Treasury so much as the doubt whether an offer to pay people for doing nothing could really benefit morale or appeal to any responsible officer as an inducement to stay on in the Service. Mr Macmillan's first reaction to Mr Lennox-Boyd's approach was to re-state some of the Treasury objections and ask whether it was not possible for officials to get together and work out something on the lines already agreed which could be presented so as to appeal to the overseas civil servants. A meeting was then arranged at which the Secretary of State explained forcibly that things had gone too far for anything to appeal to the Service which did not offer the opportunity of transfer to the direct employment of Her Majesty's Government. He made it abundantly clear that, so far as he personally was concerned, this was a sticking point. Mr Macmillan accepted the position and agreed that the Colonial Office 'project' should be formulated as a basis for consideration by Ministers. This brought about a decisive change in the situation since it meant that, while the objections to the scheme as well as the arguments in its favour would have to be presented, there was now no question of a Treasury veto.

Next followed a series of discussions between Treasury and Colonial Office officials (mostly Sir Alexander Johnston and myself) aimed at producing an agreed statement of the case and of the respective positions of the two Departments. Meanwhile pressures were building up. Lord Glyn had put down a motion for debate in the House of Lords on 22 February and it would have been quite disastrous if the Government were obliged then to confess that they had still not made up their mind. Sir James Robertson continued to weigh in from Lagos. He too was under pressure from the Association of Senior Civil Servants in Nigeria. He could not, he wrote, overstress the urgency of the matter. Men had already been lost who might well have stayed if earlier action had been taken. Others would soon have committed themselves to go if no announcement were made. Not one single administrative recruit had been obtained for Nigeria since 1954.

Early in February the Queen paid a visit to Nigeria. She saw much of the work of the civil services there and did all she could to encourage them, including a special reference to them in her farewell message. This, perhaps, had some effect in persuading officers to hang on, but the urgency remained. Mr Lennox-Boyd felt that he could not go on waiting for an agreed statement and decided to put his plan to the Colonial Policy Committee, leaving the Chancellor to submit a paper of his own if he wished. Lord Glyn consented to defer his motion, which allowed a little more breathing space.

8

PYRRHIC VICTORY

Meanwhile, the Secretary of State and his officials had other pre-occupations in connection with the Overseas Service. The Malayan constitutional conference met in London on 18 January 1956 and went on until 6 February. It ended with a firm recommendation that Malaya should receive full independence in August 1957. The conference paid much attention to the question of the public services. Following the precedent of other countries, it was agreed that an independent Public Service Commission, with executive powers, should be established to manage the civil services in accordance with 'traditional service principles'. The conference expressed the view that, if this were done, a large proportion of the expatriate officers would be happy to stay on. They recognized, however, that there would be a fundamental variation of the conditions under which a large section of the public service was recruited, and that such officers should have the right to an opportunity to leave the Service on appropriate terms.

The question what terms were appropriate involved a good deal of discussion and bargaining between the Colonial Office people and the Malayan delegation, with representatives of the Malayan public services, who had come to London to watch the interests of their colleagues, hovering on the touchline. It was agreed that a major change of conditions had already taken place in 1955 when a ministerial government was established in the Federation, but the Malayan Ministers contended, and their view was accepted, that this change had not been sufficiently radical to warrant payment of special compensation to officers who might wish to leave the services of the Federation at that stage. They conceded, however, that such officers (that is to say, pensionable expatriate officers and a few others) should be allowed to go on accrued normal pension. This 'Phase I' scheme was to be introduced at once.

'Phase II' would begin when the Public Service Commission was established with executive powers, and it was agreed that at that point a full-scale lump sum compensation scheme for loss of career should be brought into operation. The scheme would be worked out actuarially in consultation with the staff associations.

The Malayan Ministers were very conscious that, while it was unavoidable that expatriate officers should be allowed to go, if they wished, with compensation, it was strongly in the interest of their country that a considerable number should stay on, at least until adequate supplies of qualified Malayan staffs should become available. They took a very responsible view of the problem and discussions between them and the Colonial Office led to certain important decisions. It was recognized that (as in Nigeria) the thing which worried officers most and disposed them to get out while the going was good was a sense of insecurity. The conference devised an ingenious plan for dealing with this problem. The Public Service Commission would be established on 1 July 1957 and the compensation scheme introduced on the same date. The Federation Government would assure the public service that until the compensation scheme was introduced no officer would have his services dispensed with except in accordance with traditional service principles. Meanwhile, every pensionable expatriate officer would be asked to say whether he wished to be kept on after 1 July 1957. If he answered yes, his case would be considered and he would be informed of the minimum period for which he might expect, subject to health and efficiency, to be retained. The periods would naturally vary according to the circumstances of each individual; but, while the officer would keep his right to retire under the compensation scheme, the Federation Government would not, for its part, exercise the right, except on traditional service principles, to retire any officer during any period for which he had been promised employment.

While hoping that these measures would help to prevent a damaging exodus of experienced officers in the immediate future, the Ministers also had to look ahead to some years during which it would be necessary to recruit staff from outside to fill vacancies for which local candidates were not as yet available. They made it clear that they would much rather get such staff by secondment than on contract or pensionable appointment; but secondment implied the existence of a parent body from which officers could be lent, and the Ministers recorded their hope that arrangements could be made by Her Majesty's Government for the creation of a central pool for this purpose.*

Thus, although the Malayan negotiations were not very relevant to the question of affording existing members of HMOCS an opportunity of transferring, via the Special Division, to the service of the British Government, they did strongly reinforce the Colonial Office case for a Britain-based pool of skilled staffs available for lending to overseas governments as required. In fact it was this long-term and constructive aspect of the Colonial Office scheme which seems to have most impressed the Colonial Policy Committee of the Cabinet when they con-

*Cmd 9714, 1956, *Report by the Federation of Malaya Constitutional Conference.*

sidered the matter on 23 February, for their instructions to officials were to draw up the heads of a plan for creating a central pool of officers recruited and employed by the United Kingdom Government who could be seconded as required for service overseas. In so deciding, Ministers were doubtless influenced by evidence of a reviving interest, in political circles, in the idea of a 'Commonwealth Service'.

According to the rules of Whitehall procedure, now that the future of the Colonial Service had become a Cabinet matter, the focus of discussion shifted from the Treasury to the Cabinet Office, and a working party was quickly convened by the Secretary to the Cabinet, Sir Norman Brook (afterwards Lord Normanbrook). The Treasury and Colonial Office were requested to get together once again and produce a scheme complying with Ministers' instructions. All went to work with a will, and an agreed formula was drawn up early in March. This formula was to apply to expatriate pensionable officers in any territory designated by Her Majesty's Government with the agreement of the local government. During a period of five years (or other agreed period), any such officer under the age of fifty would be entitled to apply for transfer to the service of Her Majesty's Government as a member of the Special Division of HMOCS. If accepted, he would continue to serve on his existing pension terms, the pensions, etc., to be paid by Her Majesty's Government and recovered from the overseas government. The officer would if possible be given employment up to the age of fifty; if this should prove to be impracticable, he would receive whatever compensation he would have received if he had remained in the service of the overseas government, half being paid by that government and half by the British Government. (This last provision was proposed by the Colonial Office, and accepted, albeit with some reluctance, by the Treasury, as an inducement to overseas governments both to agree to the scheme, in so far as it would relieve them of a substantial part of their liability for compensation, and to refrain from lightly exercising their right to terminate an officer's service because of the contingent liability that would remain.) For its part, the overseas government would be expected to give a year's notice to return an officer from secondment and, during his employment, to provide salaries and other conditions as agreed with Her Majesty's Government.

The reactions of the Governor-General of Nigeria, when he was informally consulted about this formula, were favourable, but he pointed out that speed was the first essential. Promising young officers were leaving at what he described as an alarming rate. If the scheme were applied to Nigeria it must be to the whole country; there could be no question now of deferring action with regard to the Northern Region as had at one time been suggested.

On the London front, also, speed was essential, for, although the necessity for an announcement in the House of Lords had been temporarily staved off, the Secretary of State was absolutely committed to making a statement before Parliament rose for the Whitsun recess towards the end of May. When Sir Norman Brook's working party considered the formula put up by the Treasury and the Colonial Office, it was pointed out that, while this provided for the problem of the Special List, which was the most urgent and grave, it did not cover the question of the central pool, which was in the long run the most important and far-reaching, and, at the same time, the aspect of the matter over which the Treasury naturally found most difficulty. They had been obliged to concede the principle of direct employment by Her Majesty's Government in order to save the situation in Nigeria, but they maintained their reluctance to contemplate anything in the nature of a new kind of home-based Service. They would have preferred that whatever was done should take the form of setting up some sort of 'flying squad', immediate action being limited to the compilation of a register of British civil servants and others who would be available to be called upon as required.

The Colonial Office did not feel that this went far enough. They were willing to agree that a start should be made by compiling a register but urged that it should be specifically stated that if the scale and nature of the requests for staff went beyond the possibility of being met by *ad hoc* recourse to the register provision would be made for building up a regular establishment.

When the officials' report was put up to Ministers, Mr Lennox-Boyd expressed himself as disappointed by what he considered the whittling away of his proposals by the Treasury. Any scheme must, in his view, be applicable to the Northern Region of Nigeria as well as to the Eastern and Western Regions, and, if necessary, to Malaya, Singapore, and other places. The absence of a guarantee of employment or pay up to the age of fifty was a serious omission which robbed the plan of much of its value. He therefore sought a further interview with the Chancellor, and as a result it was agreed that the scheme should apply forthwith to the whole of Nigeria and that it should be specifically stated that it would be applied to other territories as and when this might prove to be desirable. Although unable to consent to employment up to the age of fifty, the Treasury made a major concession by agreeing to extend from one year to five years the period during which an officer could be kept on full pay while efforts were being made to place him.

It was now well into May and time was running out. The plan, as finally agreed, was considered by the Colonial Policy Committee on

15 May and accepted with minor amendments. Mr Lennox-Boyd was able to make his statement on 17 May before Parliament rose and a White Paper (Cmd 9768) was issued on the same day. I may perhaps be forgiven for recording that this was a matter of deep gratification for me, since, having reached the age of sixty, I was due to retire at the end of June and I had greatly hoped to see this question, which had been so much in the forefront of my work for so many years, brought to a decisive point before I left the Service. I was very glad to know that the effort would go forward in the good hands of my successors, especially Mr Ambler Thomas, the Assistant Under-Secretary of State in charge of the Colonial Service Division of the Colonial Office, who had been closely associated with this work for some years and was destined to continue to look after it for a considerable time to come, first in the Colonial Office itself and then in the Department of Technical Co-operation and its reincarnation as the Ministry of Overseas Development.

The White Paper, after referring to the 1954 statement on reorganization and the indication therein of the Government's readiness to consider further developments if changing conditions showed these to be desirable, stated that there was now no doubt that such developments were essential. The first problem was the prospective needs of colonial governments, as they should approach and attain self-government, for the continued assistance of staffs with exceptional administrative or professional qualifications. To meet these needs, Her Majesty's Government intended to recruit people with the necessary qualifications for secondment to overseas governments as required. Lists would be prepared of those who were ready and available to accept service of this kind and, if the demand should rise to substantial proportions and regular employment for a number of years could be foreseen, they would come into the regular employment of the United Kingdom Government for service overseas.

The second problem was the acute staffing difficulty in the territories comprising the Federation of Nigeria and the need for special arrangements to encourage experienced officers to remain in the service there, in accordance with the desire affirmed by the governments in question. Recognizing the expatriate officers' understandable anxiety about their future and attaching high importance to these officers continuing to give their invaluable help, Her Majesty's Government were prepared, subject to the agreement of the governments concerned, to introduce a new scheme. This was the Special List scheme which, in its definitive form, was set forth in five paragraphs. The first stated that there would be a Special List of Officers of Her Majesty's Oversea Civil Service who would be in the service of Her Majesty's Government in the United Kingdom and be seconded to the employing government. Secondly,

officers, while seconded, would serve on salaries and conditions prescribed by Her Majesty's Government after consultation with the employing government. Their pensions and any compensation payments
would be paid to them by Her Majesty's Government and recovered
from the employing government. Thirdly, the employing government
would be asked to agree not to terminate the secondment of an officer
(except in the case of ill-health, misconduct, or inefficiency) without
giving one year's notice, and to consult with the British Government
before introducing any scheme of reorganization which might involve
terminating the secondment of a considerable number of officers.
Fourthly, officers transferred to the Special List would accept an
obligation to serve Her Majesty's Government in the United Kingdom
up to the age of fifty in any post to which they might be assigned from
time to time. They would not be required to accept assignment to any
post which, in the opinion of that Government, was of less value (due
regard being had to climate and other circumstances) than the post in
which the individual was currently serving. Finally, it was stated that
the British Government hoped in the ordinary way to find continuous
employment for all Special List officers up to at least the age of fifty.
Any officer who should become unemployed through no fault of his
own would be kept on full pay up to a maximum of five years (or until
he reached the age of fifty if that were earlier) while efforts were being
made to place him. If in the last resort such efforts should fail, he would
get his pension plus any additional compensation for which he would
have been eligible if he had remained in his former service and not
transferred to the Special List.

The White Paper concluded with a statement that the British
Government would now approach the governments in Nigeria with a
view to working out details and that the scheme would be in a form
which would make it possible for similar arrangements to be applied
to other territories as and when the British Government should be
satisfied that circumstances made such action desirable.

Once again a Corona Club Dinner gave the Secretary of State for
the time being the opportunity to expound to the Overseas Service
itself a new departure of policy directly affecting the lives and interests
of its members. Speaking at the dinner on 21 June, Mr Lennox-Boyd
referred to the fact that there were then some 15,000 people in the
Overseas Service, and that recruitment was still five times as heavy as
before the second world war. As Secretary of State for the Colonies he
was really conscious of his personal duty to each and every member of
the Service. A big step towards reorganization had been made in 1954,
and now two steps were being made at once. The really revolutionary
feature of the 1954 scheme had been the recognition that Her Majesty's

Government in the United Kingdom had special obligations towards certain categories of officers. The intention had been to define these categories, separate them from that huge body known as the Colonial Service and give them a collective title. The categories had originally been rather narrowly drawn and the Government was now seriously considering enlarging them so as to make sure that they included everyone who ought to be included.

During the last two years, said the Secretary of State, the problem of Nigeria had called for the most serious consideration, and in order to deal with it the action taken in 1954 had been followed by an even more revolutionary step. He then proceeded to outline the Special List scheme. 'So long as I remain Secretary of State', he said, 'and I know it goes for my likely successors of any party at all, and so long as any of us retain our constitutional power to look after the interests of members of the Service in the territories, we shall use it. When a territory reaches a constitutional stage at which power passes to a local authority, then the Secretary of State will see that the serving officer gets a fair deal and fair compensation if he does not wish to stay on. Where local circumstances are such as to make it necessary to introduce the Special List arrangements, that will be done. But it really is a Special List, and involves Her Majesty's Government in special commitments which we cannot undertake except to meet a proved need.'

Mr Lennox-Boyd then turned to the future. When territories became self-governing, they might very well want British staff, but they would wish to decide for themselves whom they would recruit and what terms they would offer. Some governments might wish, for some branches, to recruit on a career basis. Others, such as the Federation of Malaya, would like to have officers on secondment, but this would only be possible if there was a parent body from which to second. Therefore the Government had taken yet another revolutionary step in initiating action to set up a central pool into which people with specially useful qualifications would be recruited for secondment overseas as required. This was an entirely new departure and details remained to be worked out, but Her Majesty's Government was pledged to do it.

This brings an end to my personal story but with the Statement of Policy of May 1956 the main lines of future development had been laid down, and the subsequent course of events was governed by the decisions embodied in that statement. I will deal first with the fortunes of the Special List scheme. As has been seen, it had taken a very long time, during which the exodus of officers from Nigeria went on, to get this scheme accepted in London. Many more precious months had to be spent in negotiating the necessary agreements with the Nigerian governments and it was not until June 1957 that the agreements were signed and officers in the Nigerian services could be invited to join the Special List. By then it was the old story: the concessions had been too long delayed to be effective. Of 2,000 officers eligible to join the Special List, fewer than 400 had applied to do so by the summer of 1958, and practically all of these were in the service of either the Federal government or the Northern Region. Hardly any officers in the Eastern and Western Regions took advantage of the offer, owing partly to political difficulties, partly to dissatisfaction with the pay provided by the local governments, and partly to the greater attraction of the lump sum compensation payments available to them on retirement. In short, the Special List scheme was a failure.

A desperate situation called for desperate remedies. The ingenuity of the Colonial Office was equal to the occasion, and after further onslaughts on a long-suffering Treasury a new scheme for officers serving in Nigeria was announced in a White Paper (Cmnd 497) issued in July 1958. This scheme provided for the establishment of a 'Special List B', membership of which was offered to all overseas officers appointed to pensionable posts under a Nigerian government before 31 August 1957, whether or not they were already members of the existing Special List. The main privilege available to an officer joining Special List B was entitlement to a substantial immediate advance, by way of an interest-free loan, of up to 90 per cent of the lump sum compensation for which he would be eligible on retirement. The amount of that compensation would be 'frozen' at its maximum point for the older officers. Younger officers, who would not benefit from 'freezing' because they had not reached the maximum point, would be given rebates when the time came for repaying the advances on their eventual retirement. A large proportion of the cost of these concessions was to be met by the United Kingdom government: it was estimated that the British contribution could amount to up to £1 million in the current year, £1½ million in the next year, and diminishing amounts thereafter. With the agreement of the Nigerian governments this new scheme was introduced in 1959. The response from the Service was good, and so Nigeria was able to enter into independence in 1960 with a stronger element of experienced officers in its public services than had at one time seemed to be possible. Whether better results could have been obtained at much lower cost if the concessions eventually wrung from Her Majesty's Government had been made available at an earlier stage is a question upon which one can only speculate. It is, however, a fact that, as things were, considerable numbers of British officers with tropical experience were lost to Nigeria and other countries and had to be replaced by experts without tropical experience on technical assistance contracts.

Meanwhile the general question of the future of the Overseas Civil Service had to be considered. The Special List schemes which had been devised to meet the specific problems of Nigeria were not in fact applied to other territories, but the problem of providing inducements for experienced officers to carry on with their work arose in one colony after another as the move towards independence gathered momentum. After a long and comprehensive review of the whole position, the British government at last, in 1960, was driven to do what it had so long and so often refused to do, namely to offer to take over responsibility for the 'expatriation' or 'inducement' pay of British and other expatriate officers serving in any territory which agreed to enter the scheme. In addition, the British government accepted liability for that part of an officer's pension which stemmed from his inducement pay and would pay officers education and children's allowances at Home Service rates, contribute towards family passages and bear half the cost of compensation for premature retirement. This generous deal, applicable to some 20,500 officers, was expected to cost the British tax-payer in all between £12 and £16 millions a year. In the White Paper (Cmnd 1193 of October 1960) which gave details of the plan, it was emphasized that what Her Majesty's Government was doing was making an offer of assistance to overseas governments, and that this was additional to and not in substitution for any assistance that territories might receive under the Colonial Development and Welfare Acts.

The scale of recruitment was in fact increased. There was no diminution of the total number included in each annual intake until after 1959. The major difference between the Overseas Civil Service and its Colonial Service predecessor lay in the distribution of manpower between its different branches. As Table III shows the numbers recruited each year into the educational and medical services rapidly overtook the number of administrative officers. The size of the Overseas Civil Service by 1960 was about 20,000 officers, a figure which the unified Colonial Service had never reached (see Table I, p. 48).

So, in the end, all that the Colonial Office had fought for over the years was substantially achieved. The new scheme was put into effect by the Overseas Service Aid Act of 1961 and most of the governments to which it was offered entered into ten-year agreements accordingly.

I turn back to the question of the central pool. Although this idea seemed to so many people so attractive and sensible in 1956, all sorts of difficulties cropped up as soon as efforts were made to put it into practice. It will be remembered that the original Colonial Office 'grand design' had envisaged the conversion of the old Colonial Service into a centrally managed body which would have provided the territories with staff as needed and could have been re-deployed and contracted as necessary in order to meet changing circumstances. But this had never been allowed to get off the drawing-board, and in practice attention was concentrated on the problems of enabling individual territories to retain a sufficiency of experienced staff and ensuring that the existing members of the Service would get a fair deal as territories moved towards independence. By the time the British Government was persuaded to accept in principle the idea of a central Service, it was no longer a matter of taking over and adapting a going concern; it was a matter of starting from scratch. In the White Paper of October 1960, referred to above, it was stated that detailed examination of the question had led to the conclusion that, at that stage, the creation of a home-based Service would not solve the problem of the members of HMOCS, and that to have put it forward as an alternative to the package deal already described would only have conveyed a false impression of security of employment.

TABLE III. Scale of Recruitment, 1937, 1947, and 1957
Annual intake into selected branches of the Colonial Service:
Posts under the Secretary of State's control

	1937	1947	1957
Administrative	91	226	109
Educational	14	139	329
Finance and Customs	10	23	41
Legal	33	35	26
Police	19	22	58
Medical	47	128	266
Agriculture	28	51	65
Veterinary	7	16	28
Forestry	12	12	19
Survey and Geological	8	28	42
Total	269	680	983

Source: R. D. Furse, Aucuparius: Recollections of a Recruiting Officer (1962); Colonial Service Division Records.

As for the possibility of starting anew, the Parliamentary Select Committee on Estimates, in its Fourth Report, also published in 1960, while accepting the view that the creation of a new Service would not offer a comprehensive solution to the present problems of HMOCS, recommended that the possibility of forming a Commonwealth Advisory and Technical Service for meeting future needs should be studied. However, the Department of Technical Co-operation (later the Ministry of Overseas Development) which took over this side of the Colonial Office work in 1961, issued, in May 1962, a statement of future policy for recruitment for service overseas (Cmnd 1740) in which a reasoned case was made out for regarding such a scheme as impracticable and unsuited to the real needs of the situation. Instead, the Department announced that future recruitment would be based on the principle that service overseas should be for limited periods which formed part of a career based primarily in Britain or in the service of a British institution. The application of the principle could and would be capable of a wide range of variation to suit the differing needs of different individuals, professions, and jobs, and appointments would be made on contract, loan, or secondment as might be most suitable in each case. There would be no regular or permanent establishment.

The subsequent history of technical assistance goes outside the limits of this study. Up to 1956 the Colonial Office had a direct responsibility for ensuring that the public services of all the territories comprising the colonial Empire were adequately staffed and its organization was geared to the proper discharge of this responsibility. From 1957 onwards in one territory after another, the transfer of power removed this responsibility entirely from the Colonial Office to the independent local governments. Thereafter the only actual obligation on the British government was to ensure a fair deal for the civil servants whom it had recruited. The initiative in seeking British help in staffing their public services after independence lay with the overseas governments, and the willingness of the British government to respond to requests for such help was a matter of goodwill and good policy, not of obligation. The purpose of this book has been to give some account of the way in which the Colonial Office endeavoured to carry out the responsibilities and obligations of the British government in this field of administration. I hope we can claim to have done so honourably.

Friendly critics, with the advantage of hindsight, have suggested that we could have taken more trouble to learn from the experience of others, such as the British authorities in India or the French in the winding up of their colonial empire. I would not dispute this, but such studies as the Colonial Office was able to make at the time of the experience of other administrations and countries tended to emphasize the differences rather than the similarities of their respective problems. The British services in India were constituted by Act of Parliament, which provided a definite basis for the action to be taken with regard to them on the transfer of power to the successor governments. If it was not a simple operation, it was at any rate a single one. The Colonial Service had no legal constitution and the application of any general decisions varied from colony to colony; there was not one Colonial Service problem but as many problems as there were territories, nor did the problems come up for solution all at the same time or in exactly the same circumstances in any two places. Again, the French system differed radically from the British, in that the services in the field overseas always included a substantial element of staffs employed by and responsible to the metropolitan government. Thus the issue of principle which bedevilled the British government's efforts to deal with the situation simply did not arise in the French context, and no difficulties of principle stood in the way of the French government paying officials, absorbing them on redundancy, or being responsible for their pensions. This clearly made the transition from colonial rule to technical assistance much smoother.

Whatever view the historian may take of the British government's record in the management of the Colonial Service, the Service itself will, I firmly believe, be held to have justified the often quoted words of the late Sir Abubakar Tafawa Balewa, spoken on the occasion of his country's achieving independence in 1960: 'We are grateful to the British officers whom we have known, first as masters and then as leaders and finally as partners, but always as friends.' Of course there were mistakes, frustrations, and disappointments. Events rendered illusory the high hopes and ambitions with which many good men and women entered the Service. Yet on the whole there is more occasion for pride than for regret. The work of the Colonial Service and its successor, HMOCS, was quite invaluable in helping the governments and peoples of the territories to make the difficult transition from dependence to independence. Things which go wrong make news, while the remarkably rapid and peaceful progress which the countries of the former colonial Empire have, on the whole, been able to achieve on their own account goes unnoticed. The record of the so-called civilized Powers in conducting their own internal affairs during the same period gives them little right to judge harshly the teething troubles of the younger nations.

The work of HMOCS did not end with the winding up of the colonial Empire, nor has it ended yet. Many officers stayed on to give valued advice and assistance to the newly independent administrations. Others were absorbed into the Foreign and Commonwealth Service. Others again continue to serve the much reduced but still not negligible number of territories for which the United Kingdom government retains responsibility.

I conclude with another quotation from one who was both an eminent member of the Colonial Service and a leading architect of his country's independence, Sir Oliver Goonetilleke of Ceylon: 'To my British friends I say: Look on your handiwork and rejoice.'

PRINCIPAL DOCUMENTS

Official Publications

Cmd 3554, 1930 *The System of Appointment to the Colonial Office and the Colonial Service*
RDW/6, 1945 *Post-War Opportunities in the Colonial Service*
Col. 197, 1946 *Organisation of the Colonial Service*
Col. 198, 1946 *Post-War Training for the Colonial Service*
Col. 209, 1947 *Civil Services of British West Africa*
Col. 222, 1948 *Civil Services of Northern Rhodesia and Nyasaland*
Col. 223, 1948 *Civil Services of Kenya, Uganda, Tanganyika & Zanzibar*
CSR 1 etc, 1950 onwards *Appointments in H.M. Colonial Service*
Col. 306, 1954 *Reorganisation of the Colonial Service*
Cmd 9768, 1956 *Her Majesty's Oversea Civil Service*
Cmnd 497, 1958 *Her Majesty's Oversea Civil Service (Nigeria)*
Cmnd 1193, 1960 *Service with Overseas Governments*
Cmnd 1740, 1962 *Recruitment for Service Overseas*
HMSO, 1964 *Colonial Research, 1940–1960*

Other Publications

R. D. Furse, *Aucuparius* (London, 1962).
Robert Heussler, *Yesterday's Rulers* (Syracuse NY, 1963).
—, *The British in Northern Nigeria* (London, 1968).
Charles Jeffries, *The Colonial Empire and its Civil Service* (Cambridge, 1938).
—, *Partners for Progress* (London, 1949).
—, *The Colonial Police* (London, 1952).
—, *The Colonial Office* (London, 1956).
—, *Transfer of Power* (London, 1960).
J. M. Lee, *Colonial Development and Good Government* (London, 1967).
A. R. Thomas, 'The Development of the Overseas Civil Service', *Public Administration*, vol. 35 (Winter 1958), pp. 319–33.
Kenneth Roberts-Wray, *The Rise and Fall of the British Empire* (Nottingham, 1969).
J. R. Symonds, *The British and Their Successors* (London, 1966).
—, 'Reflections on Localisation', *Journal of Commonwealth Political Studies*, vol. ii, no. 3 (November, 1964), pp. 219–34.

UNIFIED BRANCHES OF THE COLONIAL SERVICE, WITH DATES OF ESTABLISHMENT

Colonial Administrative Service	1932
Colonial Agricultural Service	1935
Colonial Audit Service	1910
Colonial Chemical Service	1938
Colonial Civil Aviation Service	1948
Colonial Customs Service	1938
Colonial Education Service	1937
Colonial Engineering Service	1945
Colonial Forest Service	1935
Colonial Geological Survey Service	1938
Colonial Legal Service	1933
Colonial Medical Service	1934
Colonial Mines Service	1938
Colonial Police Service	1937
Colonial Postal Service	1938
Colonial Prisons Service	1936
Colonial Research Service	1949
Colonial Survey Service	1938
Colonial Veterinary Service	1935
Queen Elizabeth's Colonial Nursing Service	1940

SOURCES FOR STATISTICS, TABLES I AND II, PP. 48 AND 82

(a) The estimates in Table I were arrived at by counting the names of expatriate officers in the Administrative Service from *Annual Staff Lists* in each territory

	1947	1957
West Africa		
Nigeria	468	521
Gold Coast	149	122
Sierra Leone	55	60
Gambia	18	25
	690	728
East and Central Africa		
Kenya	193	350
Uganda	84	130
Tanganyika	194	252
Zanzibar	17	10
Northern Rhodesia	160	210
Nyasaland	52	102
	700	1,054
Southeast Asia		
Malaya ⎱	216	218
Singapore ⎰		32
North Borneo	23	50
Sarawak	25	50
	264	350
Rest of the Empire: estimates based on the proportion of administrative officers recruited	140	230
All other posts: estimates based on the proportion of total recruitment	(about) 9,210	(about) 15,640

(b) Table II was constructed from the calculations set out below. These were derived from *Progress Reports: Appointments and Vacancies Situation* (Form A—consolidated), an annual return made in the Colonial Service Division of the Colonial Office

	Administrative Posts			Unfilled Vacancies All Other Posts			All Posts		
	Vacancies	Unfilled	%	Vacancies	Unfilled	%	Vacancies	Unfilled	%
1951									
West Africa	77	26	34	596	279	47	673	305	45
East & Central Africa	117	43	37	713	263	37	830	306	37
Southeast Asia	92	21	23	517	246	48	609	267	44
Rest	19	5	26	253	105	41	272	110	40
	305	95	31	2,079	893	43	2,384	988	41
1953									
West Africa	80	41	51	650	347	53	730	388	53
East & Central Africa	91	38	42	783	318	41	874	356	41
Southeast Asia	48	13	27	404	158	39	452	171	38
Rest	17	5	29	202	128	63	219	133	61
	236	97	41	2,039	951	47	2,275	1,048	46
1955									
West Africa	109	91	83	963	512	56	1,072	603	53
East & Central Africa	157	97	62	989	443	45	1,146	540	47
Southeast Asia	11	3	27	314	136	43	325	139	43
Rest	26	12	46	424	182	43	450	194	43
	303	203	57	2,690	1,273	47	2,993	1,376	49